ABOUT THE AUTHORS

Milburn Pennybags, The Rich Uncle, is the leading expert on the world's most popular board game, MONOPOLY — and has been since 1936! Often called "The MONOPOLY Man" or "The Chairman of the Board," the venerable financier has here consented to share his secrets for the very first time. Born in Atlantic City (in a year Mr. Pennybags chooses not to specify), he still lives nearby with wife Madge, who frequently babysits nephews Andy, Randy, and Sandy.

Philip Orbanes has made the games business his career, spurred on by his very first encounter with MONOPOLY at age eight. A graduate of Case Institute of Technology, he is currently Senior Vice President of Research and Development at Parker Brothers, and frequently serves as Chief Judge at National and World MONOPOLY tournaments. He is married and has two teenaged MONOPOLY players at home.

THE MONOPOLY®
COMPANION

by

RICH UNCLE PENNYBAGS

as told to

PHILIP ORBANES

BOB ADAMS, INC.
PUBLISHERS

Published by
Bob Adams, Inc.
840 Summer Street
Boston MA 02127

Cover design by Giselle deGuzman.

Original art by Jack McMahon.

ISBN: 1-55850-950-X

Manufactured in the United States of America.

for
Anna, Phil,
and Anita

Acknowledgments

The Rich Uncle wishes to thank the following friends and associates for all their help in the preparation of this book: Randolph and Robert B. M. Barton, Oliver Howes, Judy Willis, Anna and Kathryn Orbanes, Laura Lemiesz, Pat McGovern, Evelyn Couco, Janine Giglio, George Fox, Louis Vanne, Neil Sumner, Bill Conlon, Tony Lemone, Rene Soriano, Harvey Macomber, Donna Whitney, Sheryl F. Schulz, Sid Sackson, and the Victoria Management Company.

He also would like to express a note of thanks to Madge for her patience through the years, and to nephews Andy, Randy, and Sandy for their enthusiasm over the gameboards.

Philip Orbanes would like to thank Bunny and Bea for that memorable first game, as well as Philip and Julian for their encouragement — and to extend best wishes to future champ Matthew and mentor Donna.

FOREWORD

My grandfather, George S. Parker, first introduced me to The Rich Uncle — Milburn Pennybags — when I was a toddler in the mid-1930's. I liked him from the start. My father, Robert B. M. Barton, was president of Parker Brothers at the time and the word "monopoly" was heard as frequently in our household back then as it was when I became president of the firm in 1973.

Though I retired in 1984, Pennybags is still going strong, vowing *never* to retire! Since his first association with MONOPOLY in 1936, Pennybags has become known and appreciated by millions. Today, he and the game are synonymous. Take it from me, Pennybags knows this great game inside and out. Yet, until now, his knowledge has gone untapped.

Now we have Phil Orbanes to thank for finally persuading this legendary character to take the time to share his wit and wisdom with us all. A friend of mine for many years, Phil is a longtime admirer of both MONOPOLY and Pennybags.

So is Jack McMahon, who first became an official portrait artist of The Rich Uncle in 1961. With

Pennybags' consent, Jack has prepared a series of splendid new illustrations to grace his book. So, sit back, relax and read everything you ever wanted to know about the world's most popular board game.

Oh yes — when you're done, don't forget to tuck the book under the platform of your MONOPOLY set. It's designed to fit there so you can refer to it whenever you play.

That's why The Rich Uncle has named it THE MONOPOLY COMPANION!

Randolph P. Barton
Former President
Parker Brothers

TABLE OF CONTENTS

ONE
HOW IT ALL BEGAN

AN UNEXPECTED INVITATION

The phone rang early one Saturday morning. My wife, up earlier than me as usual, picked up the receiver in the bedroom and said hello. I opened one eye just wide enough to see the look of amazement consuming her face.

"It's him!" she whispered hoarsely. "Here, take the phone!"

"Who?" I protested, now up on one elbow.

"Pennybags. The MONOPOLY Man!"

In disbelief, I bolted out of bed and juggled the phone as she handed it to me. I raised the receiver to my ear.

"Hello. . .?"

A vibrant, authoritative voice addressed me. "And good morning to you. Young man, you've been as determined as anyone and what you had to say in your last letter found favor with me."

There was a pause. Obviously, it was my turn to speak.

"You mean you'll grant the interview?"

"Did you ask for anything else?"

"No," I replied feeling slightly foolish, my last wave of drowsiness subsiding. "The interview is all I need. It would be a great honor."

"I know," he replied — confirming his reputation for self-assurance and confidence.

"The time is right," he went on, "to tell the whole story about the MONOPOLY game. And to give everyone a chance to learn what I know about it, which is,

frankly, everything. Young man, how soon can you get
to Atlantic City?"

The small commuter airliner touched down at
Bader Field just outside of the city proper.

I found a cab waiting and jumped inside. I un-
folded the piece of paper in my jacket pocket and called
out our destination. The driver turned and smiled —
he was an old-timer with an unruly fringe of white
hair surrounding a battered fishing cap.

"Pennybags place, eh, bub? He's loaded, ain't he?
Got his picture on all those game boxes. I've seen him
in those TV commercials, too. Yes, indeed, that man's in
tall cotton."

"Do you know much about him?" I asked as we
pulled onto Route 40. Ahead loomed the famous
skyline, topped by the glittering casino-hotels.

"Nah, but I know all about the game. I'll tell you
my secrets if ya want."

"Please do," I said as we drove over a bridge and
entered the city.

Approximately 100 million MONOPOLY
sets have been sold worldwide.

"Well, ya gotta buy Free Parking cause all the money goes there. And always get immunity when you make a trade. Oh yeah, and don't forget — you can't build hotels until the little hat lands on GO twice in a row."

I was about to question his technique further when I noticed that we'd made a sharp turn onto Ventnor Avenue. The tall buildings began to recede behind me. I gave the address again. "It's in Marvin Gardens," I offered helpfully.

"I know where it is. And it ain't Mar-*vin* Gardens. It's Mar-*ven*. With an "e". It's outside the city proper. There ain't no such thing as Mar-*vin* Gardens."

His last comment, as it turned out, was the only fact he had gotten straight about the game.

"Nah," he continued, "we never had no Mar-vin Gardens. That fella who thought up the game, he got it spelled wrong. Charles Darwin, his name was. There's a plaque for him on the Boardwalk."

"I believe his name was Charles Darrow. Charles Darwin was a scientist who had something to do with evolution, wasn't he?"

"Darrow, Derwin, Doorwin; something like that, yeah. Well, here we are!"

We slowed and pulled into the drive of one of the stately homes of brick and stucco. "Went past here a dozen times," the driver said as I paid. "Never dropped anyone off here before. Don't know *what* exactly you're going to find in there."

The cab zoomed away. I summoned my courage and knocked on the door.

There he stood: the Rich Uncle. I looked down to accept his hand, charmed by the twinkle in his blue eyes and the grin peeking out beneath the outrageous mustache and rosy cheeks.

"Come in, come in," he said. "This way. Have a seat. I have many homes, but this is the most appropriate one to hold a conversation about MONOPOLY." A dog's bark interrupted him; a little black-haired terrier dashed into the foyer. Pennybags scooped him up in one hand and held him across his forearm. "Scotty, say hello to our guest."

Pennybags led me into a walnut paneled library with shelves sporting hundreds of books. Everywhere, I saw photos that the Rich Uncle had of himself. Pennybags was shaking Charles Darrow's hand in one; he was kissing the hand of Miss America in another. Dozens of MONOPOLY games filled a hardwood cabinet whose doors were made of beveled glass.

He must have noticed me admiring his collection. "I have a copy of every edition," he noted as we sat down. "I especially like the newer sets — my picture's on the cover." He laughed heartily. Scotty took advantage of the moment and escaped from his grasp. The dog barked happily and raced out of the library.

A pleasant woman in a long dress entered with a tray of drinks. I was introduced to Madge Pennybags. I couldn't help noticing that the sturdy woman was several inches taller than her husband.

We exchanged a few polite words; Mrs. Pennybags handed a glass to me and to the nattily-dressed gentleman seated across from me. "Now Milburn, you be good and don't talk this nice fellow's ear off."

"I'm afraid I've got him cornered, Madge," said the Rich Uncle.

"I'm a willing prisoner," I admitted, smiling.

"Don't let him sidetrack you," Madge warned. "He'll tell you he's the only thing that matters about MONOPOLY." Pennybags laughed and winked at her; she turned and walked out of the library.

"Well. I imagine the best place to start is at the beginning," Pennybags said, settling back in his ample leather armchair. "Tell me. Do you know how MONOPOLY got its start?"

I felt remarkably lucky. We were beginning our interview on a subject I could discuss!

The longest MONOPOLY game ever played with substitutions took 59 days.

"Charles Darrow invented it," I said confidently.

My companion only smiled patiently, as though preparing to correct an errant pupil.

He looked towards the photo of he and Darrow shaking hands. "Charlie was a heck of a nice guy, and I'm glad he made a ton of money from the game." He rose and walked over to the gold frame and carefully lifted it from its perch, then crossed back and handed the photo to me. I glanced into the bright eyes and toothy grin of Darrow, a sturdy man whose balding head reflected tiny lights — probably from the camera's bulb — as he shook hands with the Rich Uncle. In the photo's background I noticed a wreath with an indecipherable message.

Pennybags satisfied my curiosity. "It says, 'Welcome to the team'. This photo was taken in 1936, the day I joined MONOPOLY. It was also the first time I met Charlie."

The most expensive MONOPOLY set ever produced was a Dunhill game with solid gold playing pieces (value: $25,000).

In 1978, Neiman-Marcus offered an all chocolate MONOPOLY set. The asking price? Six hundred dollars.

"What was he like?" I asked.

"Physically he was a real bear of a man, but always pleasant and gentle." He replaced the photo, then began to walk around the room. "Of course, from the beginning, I knew MONOPOLY had a history before Charlie started to produce it. There were already stories in the newspapers. I made it my business to piece together the real story."

I was startled. "You mean Darrow *didn't* invent the game...?"

"May I suggest," he asked, "that you listen to what I have to say, young man?"

I listened. Here's what he said.

THE LEGEND

The popular story about the creation of MONOPOLY goes like this:

The year is 1933. Franklin Roosevelt is president; he and the nation struggle to deal with the hardships imposed by the terrible Depression. Among the countless affected is an unemployed heating engineer named Charles Darrow who lives in a section of western Philadelphia called Mt. Airy.

Like most people from Philadelphia, Darrow would love to vacation at Atlantic City — the nation's most famous beach resort — about seventy miles away on the Jersey Shore. Back then, there was superb, high-speed train service from Philly to Atlantic City. It was easy to jump on a Pennsy or Reading passenger train and find your toes in the warm, white sand of the beach in about an hour's time.

However, in early 1933, Darrow can't afford the $1.50 ticket to the "World's Playground," as Atlantic City was known back then. No money; no fun. Darrow dreams, and produces a game that will let the world in on a little of both.

He places a piece of circular oilcloth on his kitchen table and sketches out a gameboard. He sets up an old typewriter and types up rules, title deed cards, and play money. He goes to a nearby lumber yard and returns with some scraps of wooden moldings and free paint samples. He uses them to make little houses and hotels. Finally, he adds a pair of dice and some colored buttons for tokens.

Lo and behold, out comes MONOPOLY.

His family loves it. So do his friends. They all want copies. Charlie consents to make them by hand. It takes him all day to make one game, and he charges $4.00 for each. More and more people play his game and love it. Charlie can't keep up with the demand, so he pays a printer friend to print the black lines and copy on his oil cloth gameboards and the game's cards. He still colors them in by hand. Production is now up to a whopping six copies a day.

Darrow thinks he's on to something big, so he copyrights the game and submits it by mail to Parker Brothers in 1934. The executives up there in Salem, Massachusetts like the game but feel it's a bit too complicated for the mass market, so they reject it. A

Mr. McDonald of Parker Brothers informs Charlie that his game has a lot of design errors — fifty-two in all! (He was exaggerating: there were actually only five genuine flaws on McDonald's list.)

Disappointed but not deterred, Darrow decides to risk all he has and go into production himself. On credit, he orders fully printed copies of MONOPOLY from his printer — the firm of Patterson and White — and begins to sell the games to Philadelphia stores and the FAO Schwarz toy shop in New York.

The games sell well. News of the success reaches Parker Brothers. The company puts principle aside and buys rights to the game from Darrow. In 1935 MONOPOLY becomes America's best-selling game. By 1936, Parker Brothers can barely keep up with the demand.

Darrow retires a millionaire as Parker Brothers goes on to sell a staggering 100,000,000 copies, around the world, of the game that started with a dream and a piece of oilcloth.

"Nice story, isn't it?"

"Like Mom and apple pie," I replied.

"Well, it is a folk tale of sorts. But much of it is true."

"How much?"

"*Almost* all of it. The only fancy in the whole tale is its beginning. You see, Darrow did *not* invent MONOPOLY — on his own."

"Did he have partners?"

"Well, in a way. Actually, it is more appropriate to say he *discovered* the game."

"So where did he discover it?" I asked. "And who else created the game? How long did it take before Parker Brothers knew Darrow wasn't the main inventor?"

"So many questions! Let's take them on one at a time, shall we, young man?"

SUSPICION

It's tough to accept Darrow's tale at face value. Great games as intricate as MONOPOLY don't just spring forth from the mind of a day-dreamer. Any game inventor will tell you just how difficult it is to come up with a really new game, especially one as involved and carefully balanced as MONOPOLY. Think of all the intricate features — the escalating rents, the limited number of houses and hotels, the mortgage figures, and all the other finely-honed values. It takes time to get numbers like these right, not to mention perfecting the basic structure of a gameboard with exactly forty spaces, precisely twenty-eight of which are properties that can be purchased by the players.

The game may seem second-nature to us all now, but isn't it curious that no other game of its complexity has ever appeared to rival MONOPOLY? That's because, like I said, it takes time to perfect a great game like this one.

In fact, it took years.

About thirty years in all.

That's right! MONOPOLY actually originated near the turn of the century.

So who invented MONOPOLY? The right question is not who, but rather *how many* people had a hand in its creation!

TAX AND THE LADY

Real estate games date from the late 1800's, but the first known person in our trail of inventors was a woman named Elizabeth Magie. Elizabeth was, for her day, a very liberated and free-spirited woman. In 1904, she patented something called THE LANDLORD'S GAME. Take a look at its gameboard, as pictured on her patent.

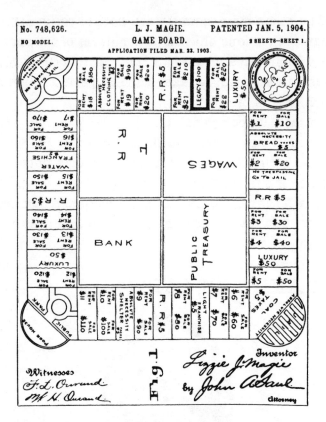

Notice the similarities to MONOPOLY: a continuous path of forty spaces; four railroads, one centered on each side; two utilities — a water and electric franchise; twenty-two other rental properties, value of which increases constantly as one travels clockwise around the board. There are other similarities: a park space, a jail, a "go to jail" space. Luxury tax is present, but not the spaces we know as Chance and Community Chest. The board's initial space, where a wage was paid, was called "Mother Earth" instead of Go.

Intriguing, isn't it? THE LANDLORD'S GAME becomes even more interesting when one realizes that Lizzie Magie wasn't attempting to create a best-selling board game. She came up with THE LANDLORD'S GAME for propaganda reasons!

At the time, Magie was a supporter of the so-called "Single Tax" advocated by economist Henry George. His idea was that the only thing that should be taxed was land — real estate. Magie's game wasn't a popular success, but she did produce it herself, and sold some copies through shops in Maryland and Eastern Pennsylvania.

In 1924, she married a gentleman named Albert Phillips, revised her game, and decided to approach Parker Brothers, a firm that had already published a modest-selling game of hers called MOCK TRIAL. There she renewed her acquaintance with the man she referred to as "the King of Games" — George Parker, founder of the forty-year old firm.

Parker Brothers Inc.

George believed there was an enormous market for games that were actually *fun* to play. Previously, board games were primarily devised for moral reinforcement, in contrast to playing cards, which were thought to be

the devil's work (in view of their common evolution
with the Tarot). Parker hit a responsive chord. By 1924
his firm had sold millions of games. When Magie-
Phillips came to visit, he studied her game carefully
and quickly realized it wasn't fun at all — merely
educational, and — worse still — political. From
experience, Parker knew that combination spelled
failure in the marketplace. He politely declined her
game, but suggested she secure new patent protection.
(Sound foresight, as we'll see later.)

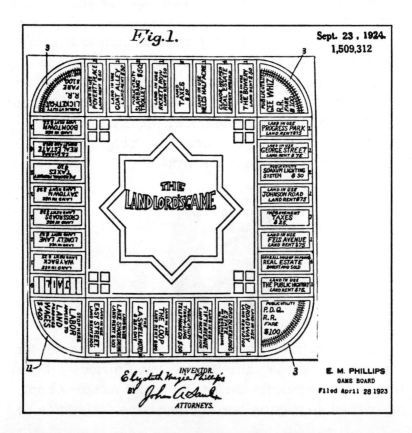

Twenty years later. Take a look at Magie-Phillips' new gameboard. She's made a lot of changes. Three railroads have taken over corner spaces; Jail is displaced; Go to Jail has disappeared; the utilities now number three in all. The remaining rental properties now have names, like Easy Street, Fifth Avenue, and Lonely Lane.

Of greater importance is a rule she added to the play of the game. Her new "monopoly" rule and "Monopoly" card granted higher rents to a player who owned all three utilities or all three railroads. She also added chips to the game. These were used to improve properties, increasing their rents.

Sound familiar?

Strictly speaking, MONOPOLY got its start the day Elizabeth Magie began to sell her LANDLORD'S GAME in 1904. While her game wasn't a commercial success, it did find its way into the economic departments of colleges, especially those around Eastern Pennsylvania.

Within these collegiate environments the game slowly incubated. It is known that the game was avidly played at schools such as Princeton, Haverford, and the University of Pennsylvania. (Elizabeth moved to Illinois for a while, and the game was probably played in schools there as well.) At one — or all — of these schools arose the improvements that transformed THE LANDLORD'S GAME into MONOPOLY. Perhaps this great event took place before the 1924 revision of THE LANDLORD'S GAME, or perhaps Elizabeth Magie revised her game to reflect some of the changes she knew were being made to her original game by others. No matter. Sometime between 1920 and 1924 someone said something like, "What if the properties were organized into groups, like the railroads?" And perhaps another person said, "And what if the rents rose when you owned all the properties of a group?" Finally, a third voice asked, "What if you could keep improving properties like in real life? You know — put more and more buildings on them!"

Voila!

So much for the noble, edifying pursuits of the Single Tax. Bring on the thrill of investing! The opportunity to make a killing! The chance to wipe out your friends!

Local street names were adopted in whatever towns the game was played, perhaps inspired by Magie-Phillips' 1924 innovation. By the mid-1920's, this bold new game became known by a new name: MONOPOLY, named after the most important feature of its play. Ironically, while many people in Pennsylvania and

Illinois remember playing handmade copies of the game during this time, no one seems to recall just who made the improvements that made the game great.

I was fascinated. "So Darrow learned the game at a local college?"

The knowing twinkle returned to Pennybags' eyes. "No. He wasn't in with that crowd. His business was steam radiators."

"So how did *he* learn the game? And are you sure he isn't your unknown game inventor — the person who added the missing ingredient?"

Pennybags laughed jovially. "I'm positive. Let me tell you what really happened."

DARROW DISCOVERS MONOPOLY

Darrow came across the game in 1933. But the game he played in Mt. Airy didn't come from Princeton or Haverford. It came from Indiana! It seems a woman named Ruth Hoskins had moved to Atlantic City from

Indianapolis, bringing a recent version of the game
with her.

Actually, a similar game was already on the
market in the Midwest, made by a firm called Knapp
Electric. They called the game FINANCE. Take a look at
its board.

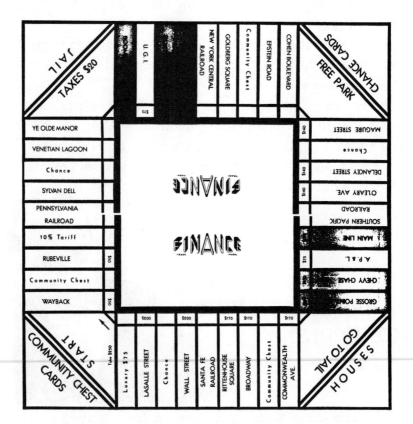

If you look at the board, you'll clearly see the foot-print of MONOPOLY. In the rules, sets of like-colored properties were called "series." "Start" was the name of the initial space. Chance and Community Chest were part of the game; their rewards and penalties were remarkably similar to those in MONOPOLY. Houses and hotels were important features of play. In fact, the game played almost identically to MONOPOLY. The main difference was that an unowned property had to be *auctioned* when first landed on — the landing player could not buy it automatically, as there were no fixed prices for the properties. Where did Knapp Electric get FINANCE? The inventor was listed as one Dan Layman. He, in turn, had learned to play THE LANDLORD'S GAME while in college, thanks to a friend named Louis Thun, who ran a gaming club.

Layman represents one of the last links in our chain. He had played the game with Ruth Hoskins' brothers, who subsequently played it with her. Ruth Hoskins made a new gameboard using Atlantic City street names after she settled into her new home. In time, she formed a circle of friends who played the game regularly, some of whom later introduced the game to an old high school classmate of Darrow's wife, Esther. His name was Charles Todd.

Todd and a friend named Jeff Raiford brought a handmade copy of the game to Darrow's home one evening. While Esther knitted (the only reliable source of income the Darrows had at that time), Charlie played the game and was completely taken by it.

Darrow had "discovered" MONOPOLY.

Shortly thereafter, Darrow made his own set. Ironically, unlike others who had changed the street names to names in their area, Darrow never altered the Atlantic City street names. Perhaps this was because he, like millions of his day, thought of the city as a sort of paradise. A previous "inventor" had misspelled the yellow property named Marven Gardens. Darrow innocently continued the Marvin Gardens misspelling on his gameboard.

Darrow's instincts, however, were good. Retaining the Atlantic City street names was a real stroke of genius. When Atlantic City was created in the 1850's, it was envisioned as "America's City." That's why the names of existing states were used for its streets. So Darrow was the first to impart a national — and not local — image to the game, much to his credit.

The colorful game board we know today is Darrow's design, as are most of its illustrations. Darrow also organized the rules and did away with the auction requirement for unowned property.

From his first handmade set, the popular "legend" of Darrow's progress with the game is pretty accurate. He did copyright the game in 1933, and take it to Parker Brothers in 1934. He began to sell large quantities of the game shortly after they rejected it. When news reached Parker Brothers of his success, the company recanted and made the most important deal in its history.

"So who alerted Parker Brothers?" I asked. "After all, there were other game companies. How did Parker get the edge?"

"Fate," replied Pennybags, "and from remarkably close quarters."

Helen Coolidge, a friend of Sally Barton (George's daughter, and wife of the firm's president, Robert Barton) telephoned Sally one day and mentioned that she'd purchased the game — in, of all places, nearby Boston!

Sally told her husband that Coolidge had called — and that she'd been most excited about Darrow's game. Robert Barton called Darrow and arranged a meeting in the firm's sales office in New York City.

Barton, like Darrow, had vacationed in Atlantic City several times. He liked the town. He also took a liking to Darrow, admiring the courage that stood behind risking the money required to produce the game independently. They reached an agreement on the spot.

MONOPOLY could not have arrived at a more critical time for Parker Brothers. By the end of 1934, times were tough for the fifty-year-old firm. The

Depression had sapped the nation's discretionary income, and the game industry had been hit hard.

Before MONOPOLY, Barton was trying to drum up *printing* business from other firms. Within one year of his deal with Darrow, Barton had to shut down production on all other games because his printing presses — even when operating around the clock — could not keep up with the public's demand for MONOPOLY!

THE MAN WHO BOUGHT A MONOPOLY

Robert Barton was a young Baltimore attorney when he joined Parker Brothers. As it turned out, he was the right man, in the right place, at the right time when MONOPOLY hit the scene.

When Darrow applied for a patent, his patent attorneys conducted a search and discovered Elizabeth Magie-Phillps' patents. George Parker recalled her — Barton dispatched his father-in-law to visit her in Virginia where an arrangement was reached to purchase her patents.

The acquisition of the Magie-Philips patents was important, because the true forerunner of MONOPOLY was THE LANDLORD'S GAME. Nonetheless, Barton also acquired and published FINANCE and settled claims involving two more similar games. Later, he issued a patent license to the Milton Bradley company so they could publish a rival game called EASY MONEY.

Parker Brothers gave joint credit, in company publicity, to both Darrow and Magie-Phillips until the patents expired in 1953. To this day, of course, MONOPOLY continues to flourish.

"So that's the way it was."

"Indeed."

"Except for one thing. . ."

"What's that?" the little man asked in mild surprise.

"You haven't said a thing about yourself yet."

"Oh, I was like icing on the cake. You see, MONOPOLY was off to such a great start when Parker Brothers purchased the game, the look of the game stayed the same for some time. All Parker Brothers did was rewrite the rules for added clarity, and include a

The largest outdoor game ever played used a gameboard 938 feet wide by 765 feet long. This MONOPOLY contest required approximately a full city block!

short version of play. They still felt the game was too long, by the way." He got up and opened a cabinet, and brought out a copy of the original 1935 board. "Here's what it used to look like — this is back when Darrow patented it."

Dec. 31, 1935.   C. B. DARROW   2,026,082
                              BOARD GAME APPARATUS
                              Filed Aug. 31, 1935   7 Sheets—Sheet 1

Inventor:
Charles B. Darrow
Attys.

"But by 1936, there was time to spruce it up a bit, and I was asked to join the team. At the same time, the treasure chest was added to the board, and my picture appeared on the Chance and Community Chest cards. A few years ago, they finally realized that I'd earned quite a following. Now they put my picture on every box and gameboard they make." He pointed to the new editions on his shelves.

"Handsome, don't you think?"

TWO
THE RULES
EXPLAINED

WINNING

"If you don't know how to drive a car, how can you win a race?" Pennybags asked as we reconvened after Madge's sumptuous meal.

"I'm not sure I understand."

He looked at me disapprovingly.

"My point, young man, is that many people play MONOPOLY without really knowing what the correct rules are. That's why so many games never end, because players throw in made-up rules that invariably make the game longer."

"You mean like putting the bank's earnings on Free Parking?"

"That's one. There are others. We'll take a look at them later. Right now, let's talk about the standard rules."

THE OBJECT OF THE GAME

To win a race, you have to know where the finish line is and how to get there. The "finish line" in MONOPOLY is reached when all players are bankrupt, save one. That player wins.

Period.

The game is not designed to make all players rich, just *one* — the winner. Everybody else loses everything.

If you keep the *object* in mind, you'll see later why so many "house rules" conflict with this goal, because they stretch out the game — making it more of a social exercise than a clear, winner-takes-all competition.

So now that you know about the finish line, let's talk about what you need to know to run the race. How long a race is it? A complete game of MONOPOLY, played by the standard rules you'll read next, can be won in two hours or less.

EQUIPMENT

MONOPOLY has plenty of equipment. First of all, of course, there are the small metal playing *tokens*. Eight silver-colored tokens come with the regular game, eleven brass tokens in the "Anniversary" edition, and ten special gold-tone tokens come in the deluxe Commemorative edition.

This means up to eleven players can play. Monopoly is most fun, however, when the game has no more than four or five players. When more than that play, those who move their token after the first four or five players have the odds stacked against them — there isn't much unsold property ahead on the board by the time their turns come around.

To start any game, appoint a *Banker*. This person should have a healthy attention span — he or she will be kept busy over the course of the game. The first thing the Banker should do is count out the *Title Deeds*. There should be twenty-eight in all. It helps to arrange them by color before play begins. There are sixteen *Chance* and *Community Chest* cards. They're shuffled and placed face down on the board. During play, they are *not* reshuffled. As each card is drawn, it is read, then placed face-down at the bottom of its stack.

There's plenty of *money* in MONOPOLY. Each player gets $1500 at the start: five each of $1's, $5's and $10's; six $20's; two each of $50's, $100's, and $500's. The rest of the money goes into the Bank, where the Banker watches it like a hawk.

Should the Bank ever run out of money, you can make up more using slips of paper. The Bank *cannot* run out of cash!

Now comes a very important step: The Banker counts the number of *houses* and *hotels*. A game of MONOPOLY uses exactly thirty-two houses and twelve hotels. (Chances are your set contains an extra one or two — that's because Parker Brothers wants to make sure you have enough). If you have extras, *put them*

aside and don't use them in play. The official quantities were carefully set, thanks to all those years of "playtesting" back in the Twenties and Thirties.

STARTING PLAY

Each player selects a token. If there's a conflict, and two or more players want the same token, have each roll the dice. High throw gets the choice.

Now every player rolls both dice to see who moves first. The player who throws the highest amount on both dice gets to move first. Play passes to that player's left (not necessarily the player who threw the second-highest total). Upon completing a turn, the dice are always passed to the player on the left of the player who just completed his turn.

BUYING PROPERTY

So — you've rolled and landed on a piece of property. Let's say you're the first player to land on Oriental Avenue. No one owns it yet, so you can buy it from the bank. You would simply pay the Banker Oriental's price: $100.

But what if you *don't* want to buy it?

AUCTIONS

A good Banker knows how to run a good auction. He is obligated to auction any unowned property as soon as a player landing on it declines to buy it. (As you'll see in a later chapter, it's generally not a good idea to pass up the chance to buy property, but sometimes you just can't afford to buy the one you land on.)

The auction begins at whatever price any player is willing to bid. There is no sequence, so players can bid at will, as long as their bid is higher than the last. (Bids must be at least one dollar higher, but usually increments of five or ten dollars more are preferable).

The Banker encourages the bidding until there are no higher bids. Then he or she announces something like, "I have $90 for Oriental. Ninety dollars. Are there any higher bids? Going.... Going.... Gone. Sold to Susan for $90." Once a bid is made, it can't be retracted. So when you open your mouth to bid, your words are your contract.

Can you name this character?

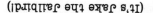

(It's Jake the Jailbird!)

PAYING RENT

The payoff for property ownership comes from collecting rent money from an opponent when he lands on its space. The Title Deed card for each property lists how much is owed.

When you notice an opponent's token landing on one of your properties, check the Title Deed and announce how much he or she must pay you. Play should pause until you've collected your rent.

Although rents increase with every house you build on your property, houses cannot be erected until you own *all* the properties of the same color. Collectively, these same-colored Title Deeds are called a *color-group*. A "monopoly" is the correct term to use whenever one player owns all the Title Deeds of a color-group.

TITLE DEED
KENTUCKY AVE.

RENT $18.
With 1 House
With 2 Houses $ 90.
With 3 Houses   250.
With 4 Houses   700.
                         875
With HOTEL $1050.
Mortgage Value $110.
Houses cost $150. each
Hotels, $150. plus 4 houses
If a player owns ALL the Lots of any
Color-Group, the rent is Doubled on
Unimproved Lots in that group
© 1935 PARKER BROTHERS

TITLE DEED
ILLINOIS AVE.

RENT $20.
House
Houses $100.
Houses   300.
Houses   750.
h HOTEL $1100.   925.
gage Value $120.
ses cost $150. each
$150. plus 4 houses
er owns ALL the Lots of any
up, the rent is Doubled on
d Lots in that group
BROTHERS

TITLE DEED
INDIANA AVE.

RENT $18.
House
Houses $ 90.
Houses   250.
Houses   700.
th HOTEL $1050. 875.
tgage Value $110.
ses cost $150. each
$150. plus 4 houses
per owns ALL the Lots of any
up, the rent is Doubled on
nd Lots in that group
ER BROTHERS

When *can't* you collect rent? There are two possible instances.

The first comes into play when you have previously mortgaged the property. Mortgaged property is "inactive." We'll talk more about mortgaging later.

The second possibility is that you simply forget to ask for rent due you (and the affected opponent hasn't volunteered to pay you). You see, in MONOPOLY, you have to be on your toes. An opponent need not pay a rent unless you ask for it. You must ask for rent before the second roll of the dice following the "tenant's".

Say you're thinking hard about a trade you want to propose. While your concentration is diverted from the board, a player lands on Oriental Avenue, which you own. You're still concentrating as the next player rolls the dice and moves. He completes his turn and passes the dice to his left. You finish your strategizing and look up. There's the Hat token sitting on Oriental. "Wait a minute!" you think. "That's my property!"

Can you still collect your rent?

You can — *if* the next player in the sequence hasn't actually rolled the dice yet. If the dice are still in that player's hand, you can interrupt play and demand your rent money. But if the dice are on the board (or even in the air), tough luck! Your opponent is off the hook.

CHANCE AND COMMUNITY CHEST CARDS

Besides the luck of the dice, the other source of suspense in MONOPOLY lies with the two decks of cards - Chance and Community Chest. They're filled with surprises. Some cards move you to specified spaces. Others give or take money from you. Some require you to go to Jail, while others give you a chance to get out of Jail without paying $50. Only the last type mentioned may be kept until used. All others are read, acted upon when drawn, and returned *face down* to the bottom of the correct deck. Again, these decks are never shuffled during play.

Here are some pointers on the instructions featured on these cards:

Unless specified, any money you must pay goes into the Bank, *not* to Free Parking.

A favorite house rule permits money otherwise owed the bank to accumulate under the Free Parking corner of the board. The next player to land there collects the total. While this is a nice surprise for the lucky player, this house rule is counterproductive because it makes the game longer to play. Why? Because the more money in play, the longer it takes to bankrupt people.

If your card advances you to GO, you collect the normal amount: $200. You do not collect again when you move off ("past") GO.

Many cards advance you to another property. If you pass GO on the way, collect your $200. If the property is already owned, pay the owner the rent due. If the property is unowned, you may buy it from the bank, or ask the Banker to auction it if you don't wish to buy it.

If you roll the dice and move your token past GO on your way to landing on either Chance or Community Chest, you are entitled to your $200 before you draw and read the card. (So, for example, if you draw a GO TO JAIL card, you do not lose your $200; you have *already* passed GO.)

If you draw a Chance card instructing you to ADVANCE TOKEN TO NEAREST UTILITY, you move forward to whichever lies closer, the Electric Company or Water Works. If it is unowned, you may buy it. If an opponent already owns it, you must roll the dice again and pay the owner *ten* times the amount thrown.

This is different than the usual rule for paying rent on a Utility. Usually, you pay based on the throw of the dice that moved your token to the Utility. Example: you threw a six to land on Water Works. You would pay the owner $4 × 6 = $24, unless he owned the Electric Company as well, in which case the rent is $10 × 6 = $60.

If you draw a Chance card that tells you to ADVANCE TOKEN TO NEAREST RAILROAD, you again move your token to the closer railroad in front of your position on the board. If it is unowned, you may buy it from the Bank. If owned, you pay twice the normal rent.

Later in the game, the most costly Chance and Community Chest cards are those requiring money to be paid the Bank for repairs on houses and hotels you may own. These cards can cost you dearly. If you have the bad fortune of drawing one, take a deep breath, count up your houses and hotels and pay the amount required.

Note: should you have to sell houses or hotels back to the bank to pay for this costly upkeep, you still have to pay based on the number of houses/ hotels you had *before* selling some back to raise money. (Talk about a double whammy!)

The GET OUT OF JAIL FREE cards are very good to have. If you draw one, or collect one in a trade/rent collection, keep it face up near you, next to the board. You may use it whenever you are in jail and want to come out without paying $50. You don't have to use one if you have it.

Remember that whenever you need to total your assets, these cards have no monetary value. If you go bankrupt, the player bankrupting you receives any GET OUT OF JAIL FREE cards you may own. Keep in mind that you should never pay more than $50 to buy one of these cards from another player. After all, this card can only save you $50!

GO

Each time your token lands on or passes over GO, the Banker pays you a $200 salary. A player who lands on GO does not collect a second $200 when he moves off the space on a subsequent roll, unless a Chance or Community Chest card is drawn with instructions to the contrary.

Can you name this character?

(It's Officer Edgar Mallory!)

INCOME TAX

Ouch! Another nasty space to land on. When you're unlucky enough to land on Income Tax, you must make a choice. You can either pay $200 tax *or* total your assets and pay 10% of everything you have. Paying the $200 is simple, but you may save money by going the 10% route. Warning: if you elect to pay 10% you *can't* change your mind once you start to count your assets, even if after adding up all your wealth you find that you have more than $2000. Once you decide to pay 10%, you're committed. In addition, if you passed GO on your way to Income Tax, you must include the $200 the Banker paid you in your count.

Since you started with $1500 in cash, it is unlikely you'll have $2000 or more until the third time you pass GO.

JAIL

The rules require you to go to jail whenever you land on the GO TO JAIL space, draw a GO TO JAIL card, or roll doubles for the third time on the same turn.

When you go to Jail, you move backwards to the Jail space. You do not collect $200 if you move backwards past Go. Once in Jail, your turn ends. (Even if your last throw *was* doubles.)

There are three ways to get out of jail: paying $50 before rolling on any of your next three turns; rolling doubles on any of your next three turns; or playing a GET OUT OF JAIL FREE card (which may be obtained through a trade). If you do not leave Jail by your third roll, you *must* pay $50 and then move forward according to the total showing on the dice.

If you leave Jail by rolling doubles (and not by paying $50) you move out of Jail according to the total on the dice, but, unlike other doubles throws, *you do not throw again.* (If you pay $50 or play a GET OUT OF JAIL FREE card before rolling, you may throw again if you roll doubles.)

Contrary to some house rules, you do collect rents due you while spending time in Jail.

FREE PARKING

Nothing special happens on this space. It is merely a resting place.

HOTELS

After each property of a monopoly has four houses built on it, you may begin building hotels by exchanging the four houses on a property for a hotel and paying the Bank the cost of the hotel. As the Title Deeds say, hotels cost "four houses plus the cost of a hotel."

You may also break Hotels down into houses if you need to raise money.

BUILDING SHORTAGES

Building shortages play a key role in a game played by smart players. To put it simply, if the bank has no houses, you can't buy any. (Remember that there are exactly 32 houses and 12 hotels in a proper MONOPOLY set.) And unless you physically have four houses on each property of a monopoly — or the houses required to reach a total of four per lot are available in the bank — you cannot buy and build hotels.

Say you've just acquired the Red color-group and there are plenty of hotels in the Bank, but just three houses. It doesn't matter if you have enough money to buy the equivalent of four houses and a hotel for each property in the monopoly — all you can buy are those three little green houses!

Not only that, but if you owe someone a large rent and can only raise enough cash by selling the hotels you have on a monopoly, you can only replace them with *whatever houses remain in the Bank.*

Say you have hotels on Kentucky, Indiana, and Illinois and you need to raise $75. You'd like to sell one hotel and exchange it for four houses. But lo and behold, there are *only three houses* in the Bank. In order to get any money at all, you must dismantle your property "evenly." The only way to do that now is to end up with only one house on each property! You must sell all three of your hotels and replace them with the three houses, collecting *half* the value of the hotels sold back to the bank.

HOUSES

Whenever you obtain the final property of an entire color-group you have a "monopoly." From that point on you may build houses on the properties comprising your monopoly. You may buy houses at any time during your turn. You may also buy houses between the turns of other players; in other words, after an opponent completes a turn, but before the next opponent rolls the dice to start the next turn. (If an opponent rolls a double, it is still his or her turn; you cannot buy houses until the complete turn has ended.)

On average, you make about $170 every time you go around the board.

Common courtesy dictates that, once you make it clear you wish to buy houses between turns of your opponents, the next player delay throwing the dice until you have a chance to do so.

The Title Deed specifies the cost of building each house on its space. You pay the Bank for each house purchased. The Banker gives you the little green building which you place on the colored band at the top of the property's space. (Once you build the fourth house per property, you'll have to adjust the buildings somewhat to make them all fit.) The rules require you to build "evenly" among the properties of a monopoly. This means you can only place one additional house on a property beyond the amount of houses you have on all other properties of the same monopoly.

For example, if you own Kentucky, Indiana, and Illinois:

- your *first* house may be built on any one of these properties.
- your *second* house must be built on either of the other two properties.
- your *third* house must be built on the remaining property.
- your *fourth* house may be built on any one of the three properties.
- your *fifth* house must be built on either of the properties with one house, (not the one with two).
- your *sixth* house must be built on the property with just one house erected.
- and so forth. . .

Later in the game, if you are forced to sell houses back to the Bank, you must sell them back "evenly," as well, following this rule in reverse. When you sell houses back to the Bank, you receive one half their normal cost, according to the Title Deed card of the property where each is located.

You'll note that each house increases the rent you collect whenever an opponent lands on your property. You'll also collect *double* the basic rent for any un-mortgaged property in a monopoly *without* houses on it ("unimproved property"). So, if Illinois has a house, but Indiana and/or Kentucky doesn't, you're entitled to double the basic rent on Indiana if an opponent lands on it ($36 instead of $18).

BANKRUPTCY

Every player's goal is to avoid bankruptcy. But only one player can win MONOPOLY. And that means that all other players must first go bankrupt.

You're bankrupt if you owe the bank, or another player, more cash than you can raise and pay. If you can't pay a debt, or make a deal to cover a debt, you lose.

If you owe a great deal of money to the Bank, you might not actually be bankrupt. See if you can pay your debt by selling your houses back to the Bank for half price, by mortgaging all of your remaining properties, or by making a trade to raise enough cash to pay your debt. (You are not allowed to make such a deal unless you can pay the bank in full.) If, after all this, your total debt to the Bank is *not* paid, you are bankrupt. Return all of your Title Deeds, and any cash you have, to the Bank.

The Banker will auction off each Title Deed you turned in. Each Deed should be sold face up as an unmortgaged property (even if it was mortgaged when you were forced to return it to the Bank). If you have a

GET OUT OF JAIL FREE card, it should be returned to the bottom of the proper deck.

If you go bankrupt to another *player*, you must sell your houses and hotels to the Bank for half price. You then give your cash and Title Deeds to the player who bankrupted you. He or she also receives any GET OUT OF JAIL FREE cards you may have.

To avoid bankruptcy, you may try to make a deal with another player, perhaps even the one you owe the money to. But if you can't raise enough to cover your debt, you can't make the deal. You must declare bankruptcy and turn over your assets as required by the rules.

TRADING

Trading property is vital to any MONOPOLY game, though the subject is not discussed in detail in the rules that come with your game.

You may complete deals with players either on your turn, or in between the turns of other players. As you may remember, you can't trade houses or hotels.

You may only trade Title Deeds, cash, and GET OUT OF JAIL FREE cards. You can't trade *anything* else, like "immunity" from paying rent if a traded property is landed on, or a promise not to build houses in the future.

The only way you can raise money *without* making a trade is by mortgaging property or selling houses and hotels back to the bank.

Players can never loan money to one another.

MONOPOLY is a game, and games have an advantage over real life because they have dependable rules. If you follow the rules as described above, you'll not only avoid uncertainty and disputes, but you'll also be prepared to play any player from anywhere else in the world who follows the official rules — perhaps even a tournament champion!

Whenever there is a conflict among players over houses remaining in the Bank, the Banker must auction them off one by one. How much is a house worth? Well, the auction begins at the value of the house for the "cheapest" monopoly in question.

Say there are three houses left in the bank. You want to buy them all and build them on the Red monopoly, but an opponent wishes them for the Light Blue monopoly. The banker must hold an auction. He sells each one at a time, starting at $50 (the value of a house on the Light Blue monopoly). A player who buys a house at auction must place it on the monopoly he specified before the auction began.

No matter what price was paid for a house or hotel at auction, it can only be sold back to the bank for one half of its stated value on the appropriate Title Deed card!

Houses and hotels can *never* be sold to another player. If you make a trade involving an "improved" monopoly, you must first sell any houses or hotels on that monopoly *back to the Bank* and collect one half their value. Then you can trade the Title Deeds.

MORTGAGES

You can raise cash by *mortgaging* unimproved property you own, at any time. To do so, you turn over its Title Deed and collect its printed mortgage value from the Bank. You can also mortgage improved property, but only after selling back to the Bank all houses and hotels on the color group.

Once mortgaged, you can no longer collect rent on that property. (You continue, however, to collect rent on any other unmortgaged properties you own of the same group.) When you decide to unmortgage a property, you must repay the Bank the amount of the mortgage plus 10% interest.

You can sell or trade mortgaged property to any other player. But the acquiring player must either repay the mortgage and 10% interest, or keep the property mortgaged and pay only the 10% interest penalty. However, if that player later "lifts" the mortgage on a future turn, he must pay the 10% interest once more!

THREE
A TRIP AROUND
THE BOARD

A RIDE IN THE RUNABOUT

Armed with the explanation of MONOPOLY's rules, I accepted Pennybags' invitation to go for a ride.

We were on Atlantic Avenue now, traveling north. Pennybags was behind the wheel of his 1935 Runabout — the very car used as a token in the game.

We entered Atlantic City and I soon found myself staring across a large, threadbare plaza beyond which a massive, yellow-brick building rose, its style clearly art-deco. Pennybags pulled to the curb.

"See that building — the one marked 'Bus Terminal'?"

"It's hard to miss."

We stepped out of his car and walked onto the plaza. Pennybags motioned for me to sit beside him on a worn bench.

"Any tour of Atlantic City and the MONOPOLY board has to begin here, because that building used to be the main train station in town. Son, those were the days when Pennsy and Reading trains ran back and forth between Philadelphia and Atlantic City.

"What about the B&O and the Short Line? Where did they arrive?"

A skeptical look came over Pennybags' face. "The B&O never came to Atlantic City, and the Short Line was a bus company."

I looked around, trying somehow to get my bearings.

"It all starts here," Pennybags continued. While there's no GO space in the real Atlantic City, that terminal is probably the best substitute."

"Life is a game, my man," he went on. "So imagine we've just rolled the dice and the game has started."

And then...

Suddenly we were staring, not at the street signs and the pavement, but at the familiar board layout of the MONOPOLY game itself!

The Runabout, now no more than half an inch long, was idling smoothly at the center of the GO square. To my astonishment, both Pennybags and I, apparently ant-sized, were sitting in the car at its token dimensions.

Two huge dice tumbled in front of us and came to rest near the middle of the board.

"A mere three," said Pennybags calmly. "Make of it what you can!"

I stared in amazement at the dice.

Escape maps, compasses and files were inserted into MONOPOLY boards smuggled into POW camps inside Germany during World War II. Real money for the escapees was slipped into the packs of MONOPOLY money!

"Well?" barked the Rich Uncle. "Don't just sit
here!"

I jumped out of the car and found myself seated at
the apex of the metal Top Hat token — which advanced, as though it had a mind of its own, to Baltic
Avenue.

BALTIC and MEDITERRANEAN:
THE POOR PART OF TOWN

It's a rare city that does
not incorporate a "wrong side of
the tracks." This section of town is Atlantic City's.

Both of these avenues wander along the inland
side of the city, several blocks from the ocean. Like all
the major streets in town, these were arbitrarily titled
by a glass-maker, Samuel Richards, and a civil
engineer, R. B. Osborne — who surveyed the route the
railroads would take to get to the once deserted island
where Atlantic City now stands.

Even from Atlantic City's earliest days, Baltic and
Mediterranean were not choice thoroughfares. They
simply lay too far from the ocean to be desirable.

As my Top Hat sat on Baltic Avenue, I looked down at the price for the undeveloped property: only $60. "There's only one way they can go in the future," I thought to myself, "and that's up." Besides, it's almost always best to buy an unowned property.

I gave the bills to Pennybags, who was playing banker from the front seat of the Runabout. I examined the deed. Rent on the property — a mere $4. I calculated quickly; it would take fifteen rents to recover my little investment.

"Think big," I muttered to myself. Rent with three houses would be $180. I had to hope I'd eventually acquire Mediterranean and build. Assuming a total of six houses, my investment would climb to $420. The $180 rent would repay about 40% of the cash sunk into the ghetto. Three such rents and I'd be in the black.

Pennybags, still idling on the nearby GO square, honked his horn and asked what was on my mind. But before I could answer, he smiled, reached into a brief-case on the seat next to him, and tossed me a folder.

In the event of a cash shortage, the bank never runs out of money in MONOPOLY. The Banker is authorized to act as a temporary "mint," producing extra bills from slips of paper.

"These are my Tip Sheets for the Dark Purple group. I've got a set for each other group as well. They're the product of a lifetime of MONOPOLY mastery. You're already on to one of the key points."

I opened the folder and looked at the diagrams.

"A picture is worth a thousand words," Pennybags went on. "And in MONOPOLY, a Tip Sheet can be worth a great many more dollars. Let me show you how to use what you're looking at."

We've already talked about one of the crucial ideas behind successful property investment in MONOPOLY — figuring the *pay back* of a group when you build on it. That's when you ask yourself how long — and under what circumstances — you'll get back the money you've spent buying or developing a property.

There are three more important points: *how expensive* the monopoly is to develop; *how often* any property gets landed upon; and the *time of the game* you can expect your monopoly can be the most powerful.

<u>Pay Back</u>

<u>Cost</u>

<u>Frequency</u>

<u>Power</u>

Let's look at Baltic and Mediterranean
to see how these ideas work in action.

First, let's talk about *pay back*. It's
obvious the properties aren't going to
be worth buying without houses. In
fact, until you have three houses on
each, you can't really hope to recover
your investment! As you'll see a little
later on my Tip Sheet, if you have
only two houses on each of the Dark
Purples, once you collect a rent, you
only get 14 cents back for each dollar
invested. At that rate, it will take
seven rents just to break even!

But the situation improves when you
build a third house on each; now your
average rent jumps to about 32 cents
per dollar — only three rents are
needed to break even.

And if you buy hotels for each, you make a whopping 56 cents per dollar per rent. (Let me point out that the 'average rent' I'm using is just that — the average of both Baltic's and Mediterranean's rents. Since Baltic earns higher rents, its pay back is really slightly higher than stated. I've used the average to represent the income you can expect from the color group, not from individual properties.)

So hotels on this color group look like a good idea — so far. On to the next measure of a property's overall value: *cost*. As you'll see, it costs only $620 to develop the group up to hotels... a bargain by anyone's standards.

Unfortunately, though, another factor — *frequency* — is not favorable at all. It so happens that Mediterranean and Baltic are among the properties landed upon the least.

There are a number of reasons for this, including the instructions on the Chance and Community Chest cards, the likelihood of passing over the spaces rent-free after landing on GO, and the number of times a player's trip around the board is short-circuited by a trip to Jail.

Finally, there's the question of *power*. This is the term I use to indicate if and when a monopoly's expected rental income will be greater than that of any other group. In this case, the question is: how long will Baltic and Mediterranean — with hotels — maintain their status as the most dominant rents on the gameboard?

The answer is fairly simple. As soon as two houses are built on each of the Reds, or Yellows, for example, the Dark Purples have lost their power — their dominance — in the game.

"So what this means," I said, "is that the Dark Purples are a powerful monopoly only very early in the game."

"Exactly," replied the Rich Uncle. "Power is a factor of timing. Some monopolies stay in power for a long time, others don't. You'll see just what I mean when you take a look at all of the Tip Sheets."

"Is there any way to sum all this up?" I asked. "You know, to quickly figure out how strong a color-group is?"

"Yes. I call it *payoff percentage* — it's what you get when you multiply Pay Back percentage with the Frequency of landing on a group. It can give you an idea of how many cents of rent per dollar invested you'll collect, on average, from each opponent every time he or she makes a complete trip around the board. Using this measure, the Dark Purples, even with hotels, earn only fourteen cents per dollar invested."

"That doesn't sound good," I mused.

"Well, it's not," Pennybags continued. "This group ranks ninth out of the ten groups."

"So these properties aren't a good buy after all?"

"Not when you compare them to some other properties. But don't forget one other benefit of owning a color group — the opportunity to create a housing shortage."

"What do you mean?"

"Late in the game, bottling up all the available building resources may be critical to your chances. It could keep a wealthy opponent from buying hotels to clobber you."

"Ah! I see what you mean. Well, it's good to know that there is some use to Baltic and Mediterranean after all. Your tips are a gold mine."

"Well, young man," he said, smiling, "they certainly can be — if you use them to help you make decisions, and not to make decisions for you. Remember, every game develops differently and you need to be flexible to adjust accordingly."

Pennybags' Tip Sheet for Baltic and Mediterranean

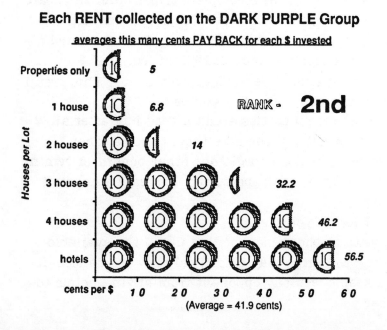

Each RENT collected on the DARK PURPLE Group
averages this many cents PAY BACK for each $ invested

Houses per Lot	cents per $
Properties only	5
1 house	6.8 RANK - **2nd**
2 houses	14
3 houses	32.2
4 houses	46.2
hotels	56.5

cents per $ 1 0   2 0   3 0   4 0   5 0   6 0
(Average = 41.9 cents)

COST to Build Up the DARK PURPLE Group

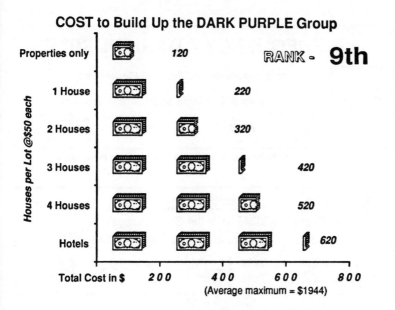

RANK - **9th**

Properties only — 120
1 House — 220
2 Houses — 320
3 Houses — 420
4 Houses — 520
Hotels — 620

Houses per Lot @$50 each

Total Cost in $ 2 0 0   4 0 0   6 0 0   8 0 0
(Average maximum = $1944)

the DARK PURPLE Group with Hotels
is the most POWERFUL monopoly if ...

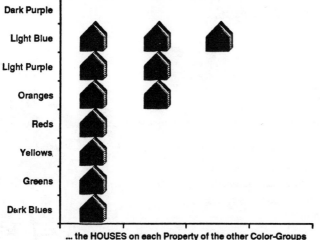

Dark Purple
Light Blue
Light Purple
Oranges
Reds
Yellows
Greens
Dark Blues

... the HOUSES on each Property of the other Color-Groups
DON'T exceed these amounts

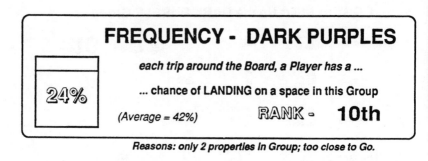

FREQUENCY - DARK PURPLES

24%

each trip around the Board, a Player has a ...

... chance of LANDING on a space in this Group

(Average = 42%)   RANK - **10th**

Reasons: only 2 properties in Group; too close to Go.

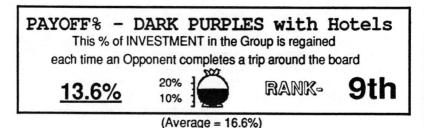

PAYOFF% - DARK PURPLES with Hotels
This % of INVESTMENT in the Group is regained
each time an Opponent completes a trip around the board

13.6%   20% ⎱
            10% ⎰   RANK- **9th**

(Average = 16.6%)

The dice slide across the board and one bounces off
the Chance deck. A five and four. The Runabout glides
to Connecticut Avenue.

MONOPOLY has to be the biggest
builder in America! Who else
manufactures a hundred million
houses a year?

ORIENTAL, VERMONT and CONNECTICUT: THE LOW-PRICE SPREAD

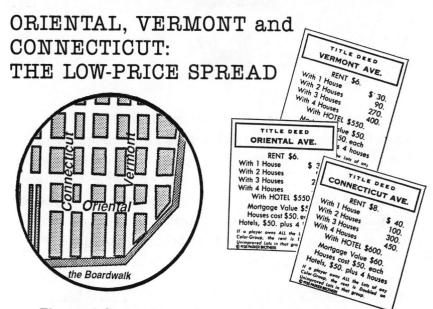

the Boardwalk

The real Connecticut Avenue lies near the northern tip of Atlantic City. It runs from the Boardwalk to an inlet called Clam Creek, less than a mile away. Empty lots on both sides of the quiet street are interspersed with modest homes and shops. A casino is visible in the distance.

Vermont is separated from its more expensive neighbor by two streets, Rhode Island and Massachusetts. Beyond Vermont lies New Hampshire and Maine. As on the Eastern Seaboard itself, New England dominates the northern tip of this city's geography.

Oriental is a short avenue running north and south, intersecting all of these streets, ending one block further south at New Jersey. In appearance, the real-life Vermont and Oriental do resemble the low-price profile of Connecticut.

Pennybags bought Connecticut as quickly as a knee responds to the tap of a doctor's hammer. "This is the group I call the low-price spread," he added, paying his $120 to the bank. "If I can buy the other two light blues and build quickly, I can usually raise a tidy sum towards building up a more expensive group. Oh yes — here are my world-famous Tip Sheets on this group!"

Pennybags' Tip Sheet for Oriental, Vermont and Connecticut

Each RENT collected on the LIGHT BLUE Group
averages this many cents PAY BACK for each $ invested

Houses per Lot		cents per $
Property only		4.2
1 house		7.9
2 houses		15
3 houses		36.4
4 houses		45.3
hotels		52.9

RANK - **3rd**

cents per $ 1 0   2 0   3 0   4 0   5 0   6 0

(Average = 41.9 cents)

COST to Build-Up the LIGHT BLUE Group

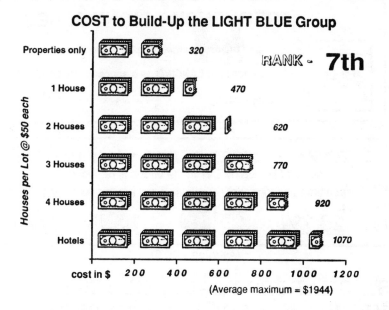

RANK - **7th**

Houses per Lot @ $50 each

Properties only	320
1 House	470
2 Houses	620
3 Houses	770
4 Houses	920
Hotels	1070

cost in $ 200   400   600   800   1000   1200

(Average maximum = $1944)

the LIGHT BLUE Group with Hotels

is the most POWERFUL monopoly if ...

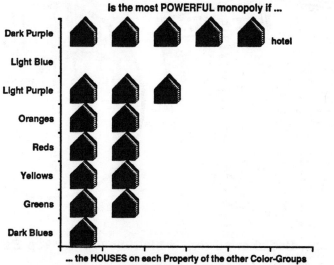

Dark Purple — hotel
Light Blue
Light Purple
Oranges
Reds
Yellows
Greens
Dark Blues

... the HOUSES on each Property of the other Color-Groups
DON'T exceed these amounts

FREQUENCY - LIGHT BLUES

each trip around the Board, a Player has a ...

39%

... chance of LANDING on a space in this Group

(Average = 42%)   RANK -   **7th**

PAYOFF% – LIGHT BLUES with Hotels

This % of INVESTMENT in the Group is regained
each time an Opponent completes a trip around the board

20.7%   20% 10%   RANK- **2nd**

(Average = 16.6)

ST. CHARLES PLACE, STATES and VIRGINIA: PROMISE AND PROFIT

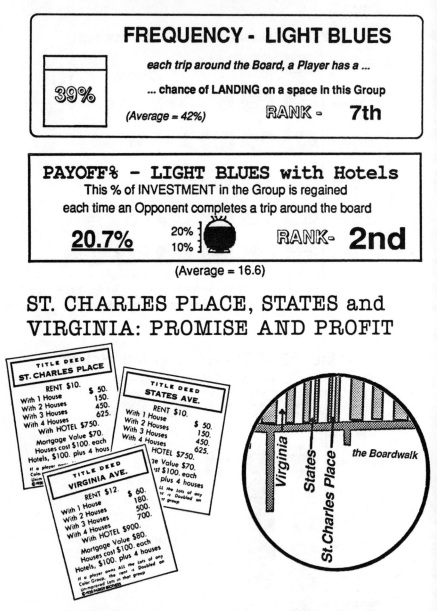

TITLE DEED
ST. CHARLES PLACE

RENT $10.
With 1 House $ 50.
With 2 Houses   150.
With 3 Houses   450.
With 4 Houses   625.
     With HOTEL $750.
Mortgage Value $70.
Houses cost $100. each
Hotels, $100. plus 4 hous

TITLE DEED
STATES AVE.

RENT $10.
With 1 House $ 50.
With 2 Houses   150.
With 3 Houses   450.
With 4 Houses   625.
HOTEL $750.
Value $70.
$100. each
plus 4 houses

TITLE DEED
VIRGINIA AVE.

RENT $12.
With 1 House $ 60.
With 2 Houses   180.
With 3 Houses   500.
With 4 Houses   700.
     With HOTEL $900.
Mortgage Value $80.
Houses cost $100. each
Hotels, $100. plus 4 houses

Virginia   States   St.Charles Place   the Boardwalk

The dice showed ten, which moved the Top Hat to
States Avenue.

In Darrow's day, this street was among the city's prettiest, lined with trees and flowers and homes. Beyond it lies Virginia Avenue, formerly the site of countless rooming houses where the stars who performed on the Boardwalk would stay. In 1921, the city had 21 theaters and perhaps 1000 hotels and rooming houses. Over one hundred shows a year opened at famous theaters like the Apollo and Globe. Innumerable songs were written about the city, perhaps the most famous of which was "By the Sea," written by Harry Carroll in 1912. The famous (and nearly-famous) preferred to stay on Virginia Avenue. Beyond its Boardwalk end, the magnificent Steel Pier once jutted 2000 feet into the Atlantic. Among its attractions were the horse and rider who would dive through the air into a pool of water far below.

I paid the modest $140 for States Avenue.

"Good choice," said Pennybags. "These streets offer the promise of real profit in MONOPOLY. They're reasonably-priced, are landed on regularly, and, in tournament play, have often determined the winner of the championship round! I hope I land on Virginia," he said, gunning the Runabout's motor.

Pennybags' Tip Sheet for St. Charles, States and Virginia

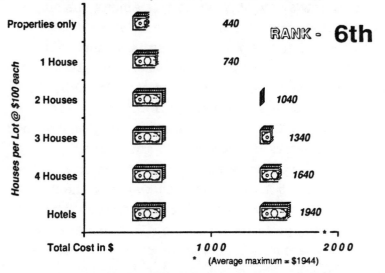

COST to Build-Up the LIGHT PURPLE Group

Houses per Lot @ $100 each		Total Cost
Properties only		440
1 House		740
2 Houses		1040
3 Houses		1340
4 Houses		1640
Hotels		1940

RANK - **6th**

Total Cost in $ 1000   2000

* (Average maximum = $1944)

FREQUENCY - LIGHT PURPLES

43%

each trip around the Board, a Player has a ...

... chance of LANDING on a space in this Group

(Average = 42%)   RANK - **6th**

Reasons: close to Jail; "Advance to St. Charles" card

PAYOFF% - LIGHT PURPLES with Hotels

This % of INVESTMENT in the Group is regained
each time an Opponent completes a trip around the board

17.7%   20%   10%   RANK- **4th**

(Average = 16.6%)

Each RENT Collected on the LIGHT PURPLE Group

averages this many cents PAY BACK for each $ invested

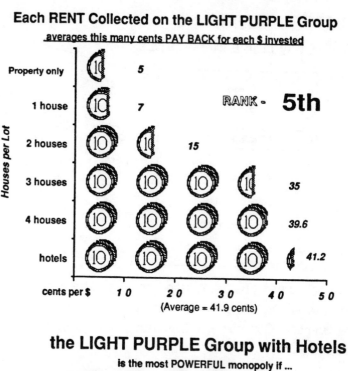

RANK - **5th**

Property only — 5
1 house — 7
2 houses — 15
3 houses — 35
4 houses — 39.6
hotels — 41.2

Houses per Lot

cents per $ 1 0   2 0   3 0   4 0   5 0
(Average = 41.9 cents)

the LIGHT PURPLE Group with Hotels

is the most POWERFUL monopoly if ...

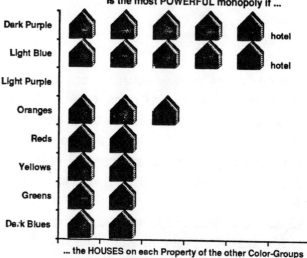

Dark Purple ... hotel
Light Blue ... hotel
Light Purple
Oranges
Reds
Yellows
Greens
Dark Blues

... the HOUSES on each Property of the other Color-Groups
DON'T exceed these amounts

THE UTILITIES:
POWERFUL PERFORMERS?

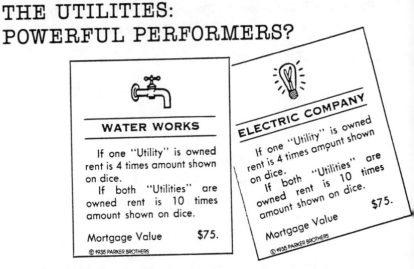

"Blast!" Pennybags shouted testily. The dice displayed a three. He put the car in gear and headed for the Electric Company, which he subsequently bought for $150.

The Electric Company was actually known, years ago, as Atlantic City Electric. Atlantic City Electric has since expanded and changed its name to Atlantic Electric. There never was a Water Works. (For the record, pipelines carry fresh water over the salt marshes that separate Atlantic City from the rest of New Jersey.)

I looked at Pennybags, who was adding the Electric Company to his assets. "Don't like the Utilities?" I asked.

"On the contrary, they're a better investment than most people think. I was just hoping for Virginia. Nothing wrong with a Utility, my boy! You may not be able to build houses on them, but they're landed on throughout the game and produce a lot of cash on a low investment. Many players mortgage them at the drop of a hat. You won't find me doing that. Check out my Tip Sheet."

Pennybags' Tip Sheet for the Utilities

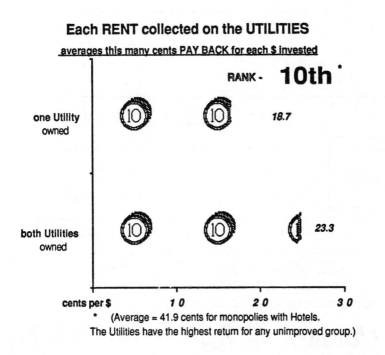

Each RENT collected on the UTILITIES

averages this many cents PAY BACK for each $ invested

RANK - **10th** *

one Utility owned   18.7

both Utilities owned   23.3

cents per $ 1 0   2 0   3 0

*   (Average = 41.9 cents for monopolies with Hotels.
The Utilities have the highest return for any unimproved group.)

COST to Own the UTILITIES

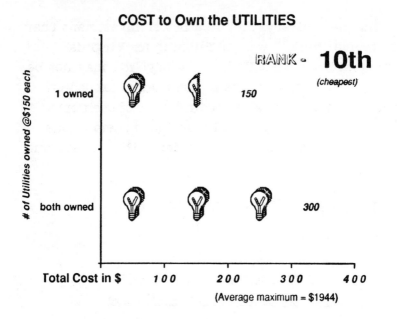

RANK - **10th**

(cheapest)

# of Utilities owned @$150 each

1 owned   150

both owned   300

Total Cost in $ 100   200   300   400

(Average maximum = $1944)

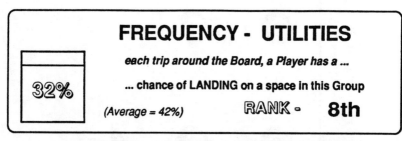

FREQUENCY - UTILITIES

each trip around the Board, a Player has a ...

... chance of LANDING on a space in this Group

32%

(Average = 42%)   RANK - **8th**

Reasons: only 2 properties in Group; "Adv. to Utility" card

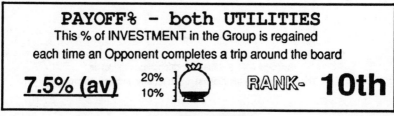

PAYOFF% - both UTILITIES
This % of INVESTMENT in the Group is regained
each time an Opponent completes a trip around the board

7.5% (av)   20%
10%   RANK- **10th**

(Average = 16.6%)

My Top Hat stood in front of Pennybags' Runabout.
I leaned forward, anticipating an encounter with some
juicy unsold property.

The dice read nine. Chance.

I drew the top card in the deck: move back three
spaces. Time to backtrack to New York Avenue.

ST. JAMES PLACE, TENNESSEE and NEW YORK: THE SWEET ORANGES

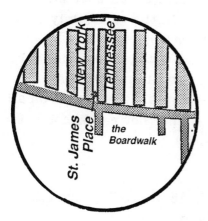

the Boardwalk

New York Avenue lies in the heart of the city,
running across the island from the Boardwalk to
Huron, the most inland north-south street. Equally
long is Tennessee Avenue, two blocks to the north and
terminating at Central Pier and the Boardwalk.
(Several blocks separate these streets from Virginia.)

St. James is but a block long, running between
New York and Tennessee from the Boardwalk to Pacific.

Well-kept rooming houses once populated the shortish street. A few still stand, reminders of a bustling, bygone era.

I bought New York.

"What luck!" Pennybags exclaimed. "The best property in the best color group. If not for the Chance and Community Chest cards, New York would be the most-landed upon property in the game. Only Illinois and the B&O out-rank it for frequency."

"Personally, I favor the Orange properties more than any other group," he continued. "They're not too expensive to buy and develop, they're landed on a lot — and I do mean a lot — and they can knock out many an unlucky player."

Pennybags' Tip Sheet for St. James, Tennessee and New York

FREQUENCY - ORANGES

50%

each trip around the Board, a Player has a ...

... chance of LANDING on a space in this Group

(Average = 42%)   RANK - **2nd**

Reasons: lies beyond Jail; "Go Back 3" card

Each RENT collected on the ORANGE Group
averages this many cents PAY BACK for each $ invested

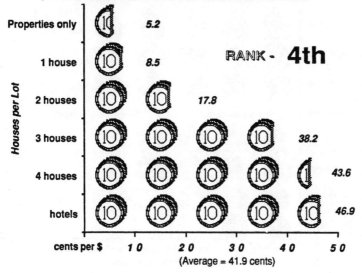

RANK - **4th**

Houses per Lot

	cents per $
Properties only	5.2
1 house	8.5
2 houses	17.8
3 houses	38.2
4 houses	43.6
hotels	46.9

cents per $ 1 0   2 0   3 0   4 0   5 0

(Average = 41.9 cents)

COST to Build Up the ORANGE Group

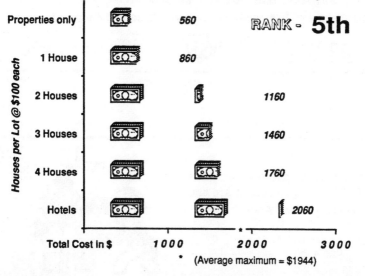

RANK - **5th**

Houses per Lot @ $100 each

	Total Cost in $
Properties only	560
1 House	860
2 Houses	1160
3 Houses	1460
4 Houses	1760
Hotels	2060

Total Cost in $ 1 0 0 0   2 0 0 0   3 0 0 0

* (Average maximum = $1944)

the ORANGE Group with Hotels or 3 Houses*

is the most POWERFUL monopoly if ...

Dark Purple ... hotel

Light Blue ... hotel

Light Purple ... hotel

Oranges   (ignore houses marked with * if only 3 Houses per Orange lot)

Reds

Yellows

Greens

Dark Blues

... the HOUSES on each Property of the other Color-Groups
DON'T exceed these amounts

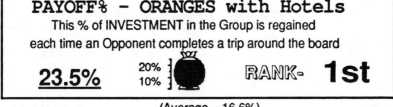

PAYOFF% – ORANGES with Hotels
This % of INVESTMENT in the Group is regained
each time an Opponent completes a trip around the board

23.5%   20%   RANK- **1st**
             10%

(Average = 16.6%)

Inflation? Never heard of it. Values on
the MONOPOLY gameboard are the
same today as they were in 1935!

The dice cascaded across the board again — nine.

"Ah, very nice," noted my adversary as the Runabout pulled into Kentucky Avenue.

KENTUCKY, INDIANA and ILLINOIS: THE HEART OF THE TOWN AND THE GAME

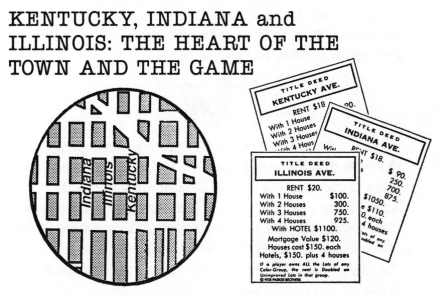

Kentucky, Illinois (which has been renamed Dr. Martin Luther King Boulevard), and Indiana lie in succession south of New York Avenue. All three streets traverse the width of the island; their placement on the board makes a certain amount of sense.

One of the great hotels of Atlantic City still stands at the corner of Boardwalk and Indiana Avenue: the Claridge. This landmark structure was slated for demolition — but then casino gambling was legalized in the city. Now refurbished, it lives again as a combination hotel and casino.

Not so fortunate was the legendary Brighton, at

Indiana and the Boardwalk. The Brighton was *the* most exclusive hotel in the city during the 1920's — many of its wealthy guests stayed all summer long. (Surely Darrow could not have afforded to stay there then.) One did not arrive at the Brighton in a motor car, or, for that matter, as a common passenger on a train. Guests with reservations at the Brighton arrived in private railway cars!

"It's only a matter of time before a monopoly on the reds dominates the game," Pennybags remarked. "The properties are ideally located on the board. Adjacent to Free Parking, enhanced by the Chance card instructing players to Advance to Illinois Avenue, this color group is visited nearly as frequently as the Oranges. When developed, they produce devastating rents."

He laughed gleefully as he purchased the deed.

Pennybags' Tip Sheet for Kentucky, Indiana, and Illinois

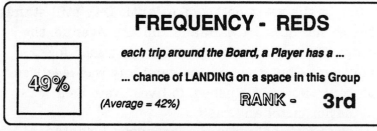

FREQUENCY - REDS

49%

each trip around the Board, a Player has a ...

... chance of LANDING on a space in this Group

(Average = 42%)   RANK - **3rd**

Reasons: beyond Jail; "Advance to Illinois" card

THE MONOPOLY COMPANION 101

Each RENT collected on the RED Group

averages this many cents PAY BACK for each $ invested

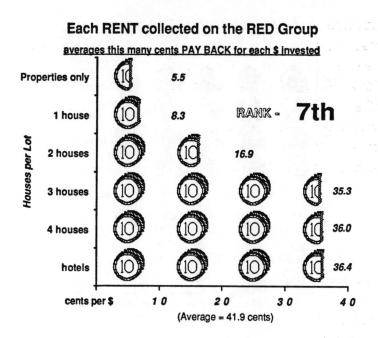

RANK - **7th**

Houses per Lot	cents per $
Properties only	5.5
1 house	8.3
2 houses	16.9
3 houses	35.3
4 houses	36.0
hotels	36.4

cents per $ 1 0   2 0   3 0   4 0

(Average = 41.9 cents)

COST to Build Up the RED Group

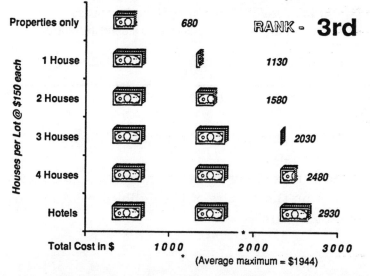

RANK - **3rd**

Houses per Lot @ $150 each	Total Cost in $
Properties only	680
1 House	1130
2 Houses	1580
3 Houses	2030
4 Houses	2480
Hotels	2930

Total Cost in $ 1000   2000   3000

(Average maximum = $1944)

the RED Group with Hotels or 3 Houses*

is the most POWERFUL monopoly if ...

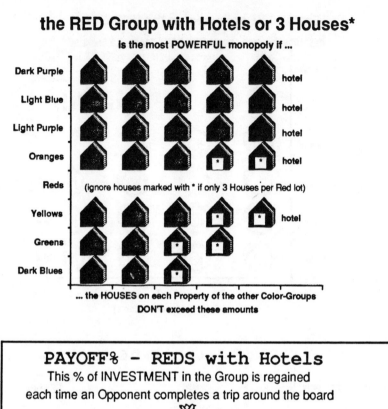

... the HOUSES on each Property of the other Color-Groups
DON'T exceed these amounts

PAYOFF% – REDS with Hotels

This % of INVESTMENT in the Group is regained
each time an Opponent completes a trip around the board

17.8%   20% 10%   RANK- **3rd**

(Average = 16.6%)

My luck changed for the worse on the next roll:
eleven. Go to Jail.

I backtracked my token twenty spaces, and set the
Top Hat atop the picture of the Jailbird peering warily
through the bars.

There *is* a jail in Atlantic City, although it is more often referred to as a holding facility. Located in the new Municipal Building, criminals are detained here until they're assigned to another location. Like most jails, this one looks cold and unfriendly.

I was glad my sentence was a maximum of fifty dollars and three rolls of the dice.

Meanwhile, the dice tumbled once again Five. Pennybags tried unsuccessfully to suppress a cackle of sheer delight.

The Runabout zoomed into Ventnor Avenue; my opponent cheerfully paid the $260 asking price.

The eventual 1975 MONOPOLY champion, John Mair of Ireland, boasted that the deciding match turned in his favor when he inadvertently dropped his dice into his beer glass instead of into the dice cup provided. Why was this mistake to his advantage? "I had to move on to gin and tonic," he explained.

ATLANTIC, VENTNOR, and MARVIN GARDENS: UP AND OUT OF TOWN

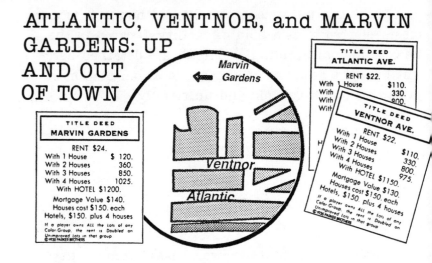

Ventnor actually becomes Atlantic Avenue just after entering Atlantic City. At the intersection where the names change, Atlantic Avenue veers east at a fork in the road and joins Pacific Avenue.

Today, Ventnor Avenue is dotted with professional offices — doctors' offices and the like — as well as with pretty flowering trees and hydrangeas, the city's official flower. Here, due to the salty climate, they bloom pink, not blue or white.

Marvin Gardens, as we all know by now, is really *Marven* Gardens. It is the one non-commercial property on the board that is not named after a street at all, but rather after a carefully-planned community nestled between the towns of Margate and Ventnor, a few miles from Atlantic City proper. Its inclusion in the game is, initially, mystifying; perhaps its elite status was well-known to the Atlantic City folk who named the spaces on the MONOPOLY board. The choice to insert the property makes a little more sense, though, when one realizes that there is no similar enclave within Atlantic City.

Marven Gardens is patrolled by its own police force. Appropriately, its space on the board is adjacent to the "Go to Jail" square.

"These are good properties," Pennybags explained. "They are slightly more expensive than the reds, but aren't landed upon nearly as much. Their rents, however, can be crippling later on in the game."

Pennybags' Tip Sheet for Atlantic, Ventnor and Marvin Gardens

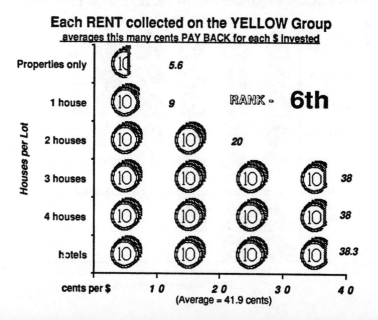

Each RENT collected on the YELLOW Group
averages this many cents PAY BACK for each $ invested

Houses per Lot		cents per $
Properties only		5.6
1 house		9 RANK - **6th**
2 houses		20
3 houses		38
4 houses		38
hotels		38.3

cents per $ 1 0   2 0   3 0   4 0
(Average = 41.9 cents)

COST to Build Up the YELLOW Group

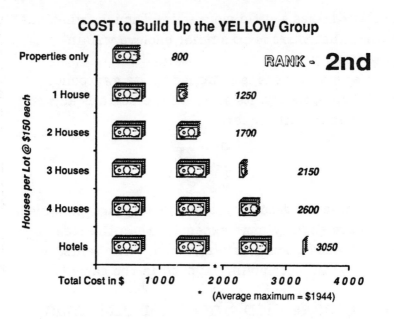

Properties only ... 800   RANK - **2nd**

Houses per Lot @ $150 each

1 House ... 1250

2 Houses ... 1700

3 Houses ... 2150

4 Houses ... 2600

Hotels ... 3050

Total Cost in $ **1000   2000   3000   4000**

* (Average maximum = $1944)

the YELLOW Group with Hotels or 3 Houses*

is the most POWERFUL monopoly if ...

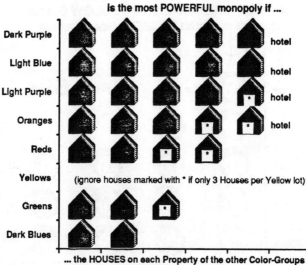

Dark Purple ... hotel

Light Blue ... hotel

Light Purple ... hotel

Oranges ... hotel

Reds

Yellows   (ignore houses marked with * if only 3 Houses per Yellow lot)

Greens

Dark Blues

... the HOUSES on each Property of the other Color-Groups
DON'T exceed these amounts

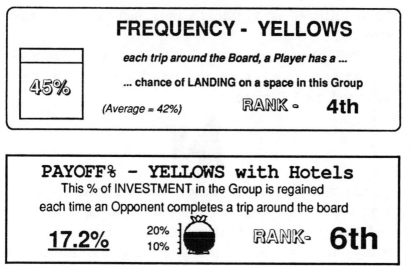

FREQUENCY - YELLOWS

each trip around the Board, a Player has a ...

... chance of LANDING on a space in this Group

45%

(Average = 42%)   RANK - **4th**

PAYOFF% - YELLOWS with Hotels

This % of INVESTMENT in the Group is regained
each time an Opponent completes a trip around the board

17.2%   20%   RANK- **6th**
             10%

(Average = 16.6%)

My turn. The dice or the cash to get out of jail?

I elected to cast my lot with the fates and hope for doubles.

No luck — seven.

"You should have paid," Pennybags said. "Early in the game you need to be in motion around the board to accumulate property. Sitting in jail does one no good at this stage."

Pennybags, true to form, ended up with the first doubles on *his* turn. Two threes. He puttered to Community Chest, unrolled the Runabout's window, and drew a card.

(Years ago, Community Chest was the forerunner of the United Way. As a civic fund-raising organization it helped the unfortunate. The MONOPOLY space in question is adjacent to Pacific Avenue; the real

Community Chest building was in fact located on that street.)

Pennybags drew a card that read, "You have won second prize in a beauty contest." He chortled as he collected his $10 prize.

As it happens, The Miss America pageant *is* held each year in the huge Convention Center at Boardwalk and Mississippi. The building is huge and imposing. It is big enough to host indoor football games. Helicopters have flown around its spacious interior. Presidents have been nominated from its floor. It was built in 1929 to bring winter business into the city.

Ten dollars for second place? Times certainly have changed. In 1987, the second place winner in the Miss America pageant won $20,000.

Pennybags, his luck running suspiciously strong, pulled yet another doubles roll out of the dice. Pennybags' moved into Mediterranean. The old man bought it, of course, blocking my shot at a monopoly. Pennybags, the first to complete a full circuit around the board, claimed his $200 salary. I watched from Jail as the dice hit the board yet again. A five and a four. The Runabout puttered and popped just outside my cell.

"Just visiting!" Pennybags exclaimed. "Glad I didn't roll a third doubles."

I didn't chance another roll without paying. After parting with my $50, I exited my cell. The dice read seven. I found myself on the platform of the Pennsylvania Railroad.

THE RAILROADS: CASH COWS

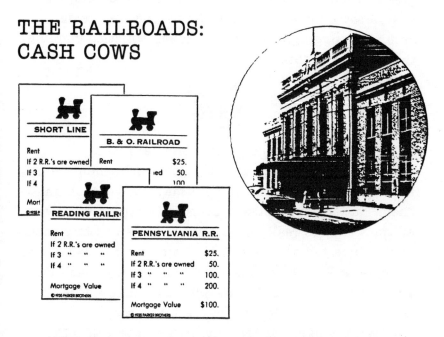

1927. Hundreds of people mill about the platform, waiting for the 6:12 to whisk everyone back to Philadelphia. Times are good. The ladies are dressed in their finest; the men wear top hats. You can almost breathe the prosperity in the air.

Today, Amtrak is building a new high-speed line into Atlantic City. Eventually, it will again carry people back and forth from Philadelphia. But these passengers will mainly be day visitors, eager to gamble their stakes at the casinos, then head home.

Trains. Hard to believe it, but the Bus Terminal that began our journey was once a grand structure: eight wide tracks; sheltering roofs above the intervening platforms; the deep red cars of the Pennsy, the green cars of the Reading, the famous Blue Comet of the Jersey Central. It's easy to imagine the steam engines chugging, their high-pitched whistles piercing the quiet of nights gone by.

I paid $200 for the game's first railroad.

"The railroads are a pretty good investment, you know," said my adversary. "You may not get rich on them, but they're a steady source of cash. If you own all four, they're really cash cows — once you buy them, you've invested all you can in them, but the rents keep pouring in, thanks to the two Chance cards that send you to the nearest railroads, plus the 'Take a ride on the Reading' card. By the way, a lot of people pronounce that name incorrectly. It isn't the REED-ING

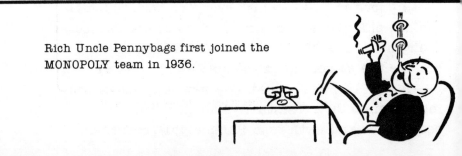

Rich Uncle Pennybags first joined the MONOPOLY team in 1936.

Railroad, it's the RED-ING Railroad. It's named after
the city in Pennsylvania where it was headquartered."

Pennybags' Tip Sheet for the Railroads

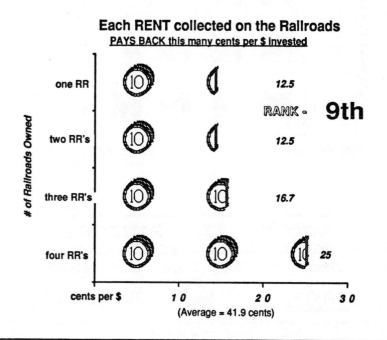

Each RENT collected on the Railroads
PAYS BACK this many cents per $ invested

# of Railroads Owned

one RR — 12.5

RANK - **9th**

two RR's — 12.5

three RR's — 16.7

four RR's — 25

cents per $ 10   20   30
(Average = 41.9 cents)

FREQUENCY - RAILROADS

each trip around the Board, a Player has a ...

... chance of LANDING on a space in this Group

64%

(Average = 42%)   RANK -   **1st**

Reasons: 4 properties in Group; 3 "Adv. to RR" cards

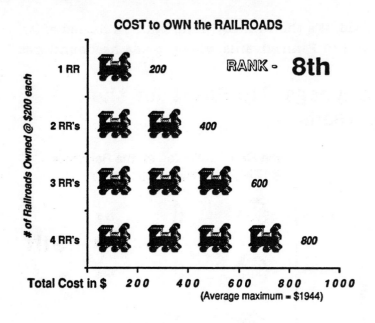

COST to OWN the RAILROADS

# of Railroads Owned @ $200 each

		RANK - **8th**
1 RR	*200*	
2 RR's	*400*	
3 RR's	*600*	
4 RR's	*800*	

Total Cost in $ 200   400   600   800   1000
(Average maximum = $1944)

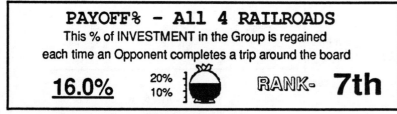

PAYOFF% – All 4 RAILROADS
This % of INVESTMENT in the Group is regained
each time an Opponent completes a trip around the board

16.0%   20% 10%   RANK- **7th**

(Average = 16.6%)

The man's way with a pair of dice, to put it
bluntly, was staggering. Pennybags took advantage of
doubles yet again — advancing the Runabout to Free
Parking.

If there's one thing you *won't* find in Atlantic City today, it's free parking. The casinos attract so many visitors the employees have to park their cars along the Atlantic City Expressway, miles outside of town. The casinos must bus them in from there. Back in Darrow's time, a very few streets in the city were lined with first-generation parking meters, complete with hand-cranked, orange "Violation" wheels.

Twelve. Doubles again. It was unbelievable.

The Runabout was off again. Pennybags hit the brakes on the green of North Carolina.

PACIFIC, NORTH CAROLINA and PENNSYLVANIA: FOR THE EXPENSIVE TASTES

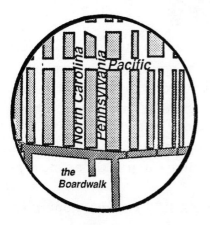

the Boardwalk

TITLE DEED
PACIFIC AVE.
RENT $26.
With 1 House $ 130.
With 2 Houses   390.
With 3 Houses   900.
With 4 Houses   1100.
HOTEL $1275.
Value $150
$200

TITLE DEED
PENNSYLVANIA AVE.
RENT $28. $ 150.
                450.
               1000.
With 1 House
With 2 House
With 3 Hous
With 4 Hou
With H

TITLE DEED
NO. CAROLINA AVE.
RENT $26.
With 1 House $ 130.
With 2 Houses   390.
With 3 Houses   900.
With 4 Houses   1100.
With HOTEL $1275.
Mortgage Value $150.
Houses cost $200. each
Hotels, $200. plus 4 houses
If a player owns ALL the Lots of any Color Group, the rent is Doubled on Unimproved Lots in that group
© 1935 PARKER BROTHERS

At the tender age of 22, John Philip Sousa performed in public for the first time at North Carolina and the Boardwalk, at the Haddon Hall — another of the city's great old hotels. Today it still operates, as a Resorts International hotel and casino.

After a fairly orderly progression southwards through the city, North Carolina and Pennsylvania break the pattern. They're located between Tennessee and Virginia — properties on the opposite side of the gameboard. Pacific intersects both, as well as most of the other cross-streets in town.

The decision to place them on the prestigious fourth side of the board is not without merit. These were elite streets in the Twenties and Thirties. Today, both streets terminate astride Resorts International — the first casino in Atlantic City — in the heart of the Boardwalk's attractions. The stately old Post Office also stands on Pennsylvania.

As usual, my opponent had an opinion.

"The Greens are far from my favorite group. They're for those whose taste runs to the expensive side." Pennybags pondered the $300 price tag. "They don't get landed on much. They're awfully expensive, so you can't afford to develop them early. And they don't pay back, dollar for dollar, as quickly as most properties."

"Are you going to auction it?" I asked, hoping to

pick the property up at a bargain price.

"With one bidder? No, no." He placed the bills in the bank. "Mind you, they can dominate if the game goes on for a while." He studied the board, then eyed my holdings. Thus far, for all his help, I wasn't presenting him with much of a challenge!

Pennybags' Tip Sheet for Pacific, North Carolina and Pennsylvania

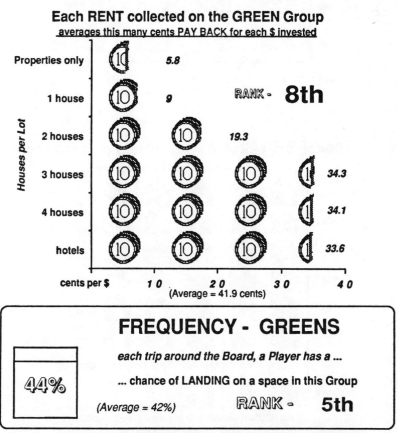

Each RENT collected on the GREEN Group
averages this many cents PAY BACK for each $ invested

Houses per Lot	cents per $
Properties only	5.8
1 house	9 RANK - 8th
2 houses	19.3
3 houses	34.3
4 houses	34.1
hotels	33.6

cents per $ 1 0   2 0   3 0   4 0
(Average = 41.9 cents)

FREQUENCY - GREENS

each trip around the Board, a Player has a ...

44%

... chance of LANDING on a space in this Group

(Average = 42%)   RANK - **5th**

Reason: location just beyond "Go to Jail" holds down odds

COST to Build-Up the GREEN Group

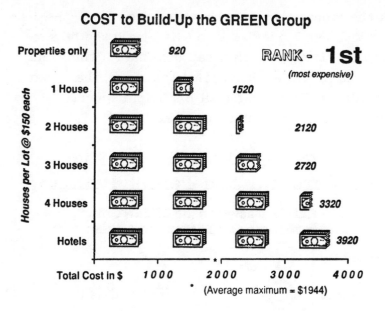

Houses per Lot @ $150 each		
Properties only	920	RANK - 1st *(most expensive)*
1 House	1520	
2 Houses	2120	
3 Houses	2720	
4 Houses	3320	
Hotels	3920	

Total Cost in $ 1000   2000   3000   4000

* (Average maximum = $1944)

the GREEN Group with Hotels or 3 Houses*
is the most POWERFUL monopoly if ...

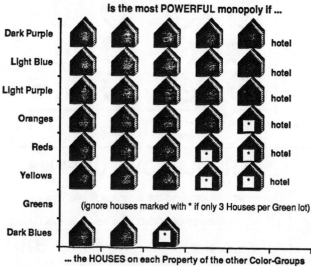

Dark Purple					hotel
Light Blue					hotel
Light Purple					hotel
Oranges					hotel
Reds					hotel
Yellows					hotel
Greens	(ignore houses marked with * if only 3 Houses per Green lot)				
Dark Blues					

... the HOUSES on each Property of the other Color-Groups
DON'T exceed these amounts

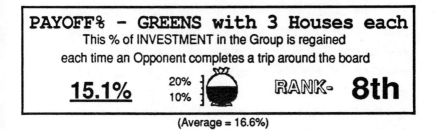

PAYOFF% – GREENS with 3 Houses each
This % of INVESTMENT in the Group is regained
each time an Opponent completes a trip around the board

15.1%   20%   RANK‑ **8th**
                    10%

(Average = 16.6%)

At long last, Pennybags got a bad break. He pulled
into the Luxury Tax space, and begrudgingly placed
$75 in the Bank.

For my part, I came up with a seven. Chance.

(There is no real "chance" in Atlantic City, except
possibly in the casinos!)

I drew the card, then smiled; the Top Hat advanced
to Boardwalk.

BOARDWALK and PARK PLACE:
THE DOMAIN OF THE RICH AND
FAMOUS

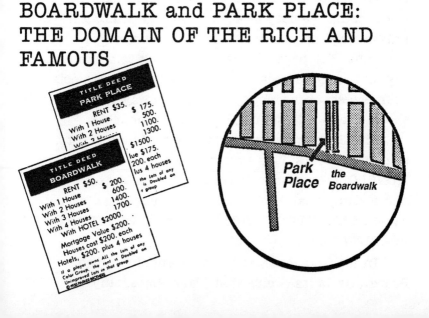

The Boardwalk was born for purely practical reasons. In the mid-1800's, a hotel owner named Alexander Boardman suggested to his peers that a walkway of wooden planks be built along the shore to prevent guests from tracking sand into their seaside hotels. The idea made sense; the first boardwalk was built in Atlantic City.

The Boardwalk attracted more hotel builders. The wooden walkway was enlarged, then built permanently on concrete piers. Soon, this promenade became the center of life in the city as every visitor was lured to stroll its two-mile length.

In this century, the Boardwalk was further extended through adjoining Ventnor, Margate, and Longport, its total length surpassing seven miles. Great piers, like the Steel Pier, were built beyond it over the sea. Eventually, its width reached forty feet! Among the dazzling variety of attractions built along its length was the inimitable Lucy, a six-story tall elephant. She began life as a gimmick to sell advertising, but in time became first a tavern, then a cottage, then a restaurant. Today, relocated away from the shore, she is a National Historic Landmark.

The Boardwalk is everything to Atlantic City, and to many players, it is everything to the game of MONOPOLY. So symbolic is its space for grand wealth and fortune that Parker Brothers introduced a new game in MONOPOLY's fiftieth year called ADVANCE TO BOARDWALK.

In marked contrast to the grandeur of the Boardwalk is its companion, Park Place, tiny by comparison. It is, in fact, a street. Nearby, on the Boardwalk, is a bronze plaque featuring the profile of Charles Darrow, commemorating him and MONOPOLY.

True to its MONOPOLY reputation, this is indeed a pricey part of Atlantic City.

"Both Park Place and Boardwalk offer high return on investment," said the Rich Uncle. "Since there are only two properties in this group, it's actually cheaper to develop them than the three-property Green group. While Park Place is not landed on as much as some other properties, Boardwalk is a more common destination — thanks to the very card you just drew."

I gladly pay my $400 and add its rich blue deed to my collection.

Pennybags' Tip Sheet for Boardwalk and Park Place

FREQUENCY - DARK BLUES

27%

each trip around the Board, a Player has a ...

... chance of LANDING on a space in this Group

(Average = 42%)   RANK ▫   **9th**

Each RENT collected on the DARK BLUE Group
averages this many cents PAY BACK for each $ Invested

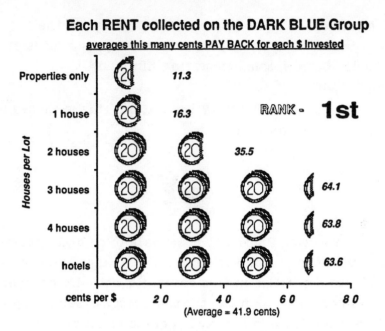

Houses per Lot	cents per $				
Properties only	11.3				RANK - **1st**
1 house	16.3				
2 houses	35.5				
3 houses	64.1				
4 houses	63.8				
hotels	63.6				

cents per $ 2 0   4 0   6 0   8 0

(Average = 41.9 cents)

COST to Build Up the DARK BLUE Group

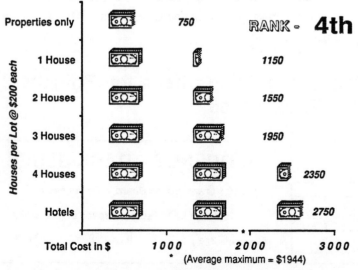

Houses per Lot @ $200 each		
Properties only	750	RANK - **4th**
1 House	1150	
2 Houses	1550	
3 Houses	1950	
4 Houses	2350	
Hotels	2750	

Total Cost in $ 1 0 0 0   2 0 0 0   3 0 0 0

* (Average maximum = $1944)

the DARK BLUE Group with Hotels or 3 Houses*

is the most POWERFUL monopoly if ...

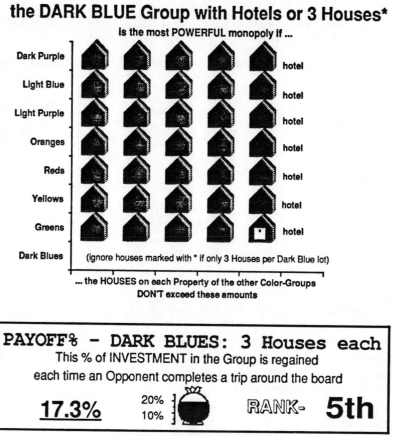

Dark Purple						hotel
Light Blue						hotel
Light Purple						hotel
Oranges						hotel
Reds						hotel
Yellows						hotel
Greens						hotel
Dark Blues	(ignore houses marked with * if only 3 Houses per Dark Blue lot)

**... the HOUSES on each Property of the other Color-Groups
DON'T exceed these amounts**

PAYOFF% – DARK BLUES: 3 Houses each
This % of INVESTMENT in the Group is regained
each time an Opponent completes a trip around the board

17.3%   20%]
              10%]   RANK- **5th**

(Average = 16.6%)

"Well," says Pennybags, with perhaps a trace of envy, "It looks as though we're both ready to get serious."

The real game, it seemed, was about to begin.

Pennybags' MONOPOLY Top 10!

Each monopoly rated for Investment Cost; Pay Back; Payoff; Frequency.

MAXIMUM INVESTMENT COSTS			MAXIMUM PAY BACK PERCENTAGE		
1.	Greens	$3920	1.	Dark Blues	64.1%
2.	Yellows	$3050	2.	Dark Purples	56.6%
3.	Reds	$2930	3.	Light Blues	53.0%
4.	Dark Blues	$2750	4.	Oranges	46.9%
5.	Oranges	$2060	5.	Light Purples	41.2%
6.	Light Purples	$1940	6.	Yellows	38.3%
7.	Light Blues	$1070	7.	Reds	36.4%
8.	Railroads	$800	8.	Greens	34.3%
9.	Dark Purples	$620	9.	Railroads	25%
10.	Utilities	$300	10.	Utilities	23.3% (avg

PAYOFF PERCENTAGE			FREQUENCY		
1.	Oranges	23.5%	1.	Railroads	64%
2.	Light Blues	20.7%	2.	Oranges	50%
3.	Reds	17.8%	3.	Reds	49%
4.	Light Purples	17.7%	4.	Yellows	45%
5.	Dark Blues	17.3%	5.	Greens	44%
6.	Yellows	17.2%	6.	Light Purples	43%
7.	Railroads	16.0%	7.	Light Blues	39%
8.	Greens	15.1%	8.	Utilities	32%
9.	Dark Purples	13.6%	9.	Dark Blues	27%
10.	Utilities	7.5%	10.	Dark Purples	24%

One of the more controversial moments in the 1983 United States Championship Tournament occurred when a player decided to reduce his three hotels to twelve houses in order to block an opponent from buying the remaining houses in the bank. From this incident forward, this tactic was outlawed in tournament play. The Chief Judge ruled that a building shortage is in effect only if property development is halted at the four house level. By moving up to hotels, a player foregoes his right to "back into" a housing shortage should other players wish to purchase the houses remaining in the bank.

FOUR
THE WINNING
TOUCH

THE ENDGAME BEGINS

"MONOPOLY is just like life," Pennybags shouted from the driver's seat of the Runabout. "There are no hard and fast rules for success, but there are principles that improve your chances. If you learn them and work them to your advantage, you'll win more than you lose."

I had finally passed GO, landing on the Reading Railroad, which I purchased with my $200 salary.

Pennybags threw a ten and bought St. James. "Now here's an instance," he said, "where I can put my own ideas to work. I'm buying St. James for $180. By doing that I take away your chance to get all the orange properties without having to make a deal with me. Since the Oranges are such a productive group, I'd rather not face three imposing hotels there, poised to wipe me out. Unless, of course, I can get a reasonable value in trade from you."

"I can't argue with your logic."

"No one can, young man." He smiled. "As it happens, I've just demonstrated two of my most important principles. The first has to do with blocking an opponent's desired monopoly. The second concerns trading techniques." Pennybags dipped into his briefcase again.

He pulled out a tiny booklet. Here's what it said.

PENNYBAGS' LUCKY THIRTEEN-STEP SYSTEM FOR WINNING AT MONOPOLY

1. NEVER FORGET THE OBJECT OF THE GAME

The object is to bankrupt all opponents. To do so, you must be dedicated and make each decision with the aim of improving your chances of wiping out your opponents.

Never let an opponent off the ropes. Luck plays a key role in the game and luck can turn against you if you do not bankrupt a player as quickly as you can.

2. KNOW THE EQUIPMENT WELL

Remember, there are 32 houses and 12 hotels. Use this knowledge to create housing shortages when it is to your advantage.

There are 16 Chance Cards.

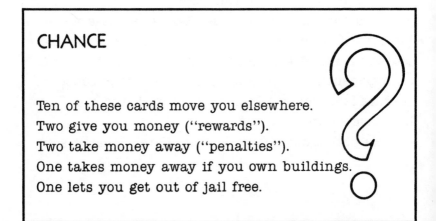

CHANCE

Ten of these cards move you elsewhere.
Two give you money ("rewards").
Two take money away ("penalties").
One takes money away if you own buildings.
One lets you get out of jail free.

A Chance card will, most likely, send you to another space.

Keep track of which cards have been played. Since the deck is not shuffled, you can deduce which cards haven't come up. If you have a great memory, you'll know which cards to expect when they recycle.

There are sixteen Community Chest Cards.

COMMUNITY CHEST

Nine of these cards give you money ("rewards").
Three take money away ("penalties").
Two move you elsewhere.
One takes money away if you own buildings.
One lets you get out of jail free.

A Community Chest Card will, most likely, give you a reward.

Keep track of cards played from this deck as well.

Know the odds of throwing any number with the dice.

HOW MANY OF THE 36 POSSIBLE DICE THROWS RESULT IN A GIVEN TOTAL?

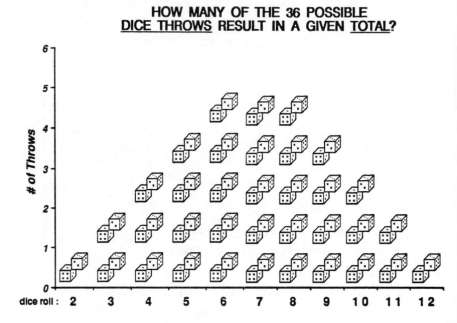

3. KEEP TABS ON THE AMOUNT OF MONEY IN THE GAME

Each player starts with $1500.

On an average circuit of the board, prior to houses appearing, a player will make about $170. (This takes into account passing GO, earning rewards, paying penalties and taxes, and the effect of rents.)

By knowing approximately how much cash an opponent has, you can know how far he or she can bid in an auction, how much rent he or she can afford to

pay, or how many buildings he or she can purchase
without mortgaging.

4. REMEMBER WHAT'S LIKELY TO TAKE PLACE DURING THE GAME

It usually takes five turns to go around the board.
Every time you go around the board, you'll probably
roll doubles once, and you'll probably land on four of
the 28 property spaces.

Count how many unmortgaged properties your
opponents own and divide by 7. The resulting figure
will tell you approximately how many rents you can
expect to pay on your next circuit around the board.
(Example: your opponents collectively own 11 properties. You can expect to land on 1.6 (round off to 2) of
them on your next circuit of the board.

5. ALWAYS BUY AN UNOWNED PROPERTY IF. . .

No other player owns a property in its color group.
It gives you a second or third property of its group.
It blocks an opponent from getting a monopoly.
It is an orange property (always block this group if
you can).

There are, of course, some exceptions. Don't feel
you must block a group if two other players each have
a property of the group and also have more valuable
groups split between them.

Example: Players A and B own all the Reds and
Oranges between them. They each own a Light Purple.
You land on the unowned Light Purple. You do not
need to buy it.)

(Counter-example: Players A and B own all the Oranges and Light Purples between them. They each own a Red. You land on the unowned Red. You *should* buy it. Otherwise you increase the chances these players will trade and develop the most powerful monopoly among the three groups — the Reds.)

6. KNOW THE PROS AND CONS OF EACH COLOR GROUP

Study the Tip Sheets.

7. KNOW WHEN TO PAY 10% INCOME TAX

As a general rule, pay 10% if you haven't gone around the board three times. (Remember, you started with $1500 and will probably make $170 each time you go around the board. After three turns your assets should be over $2000.)

Pay 10% later in the game only if you have paid heavy rents and are fairly sure your assets are below $2000.

The best MONOPOLY players can predict which Chance and Community Chest cards will be drawn. Because the decks are never shuffled, all a player has to do is memorize the sequence in which the cards first appeared. Though the task is less daunting than it may initially seem — there are only sixteen cards in each deck — it's still quite a trick.

8. KNOW WHEN TO STAY IN JAIL

Pay $50 and get out of Jail early in the game while many properties remain unowned and undeveloped. You need to be in circulation.

When most properties *are* developed between Jail and the Go to Jail space, roll the dice and hope you stay in Jail. It's better than paying rent!

This is especially important when certain dangerous color groups are heavily developed (Orange, for instance). By staying in Jail you avoid the chance of landing on such a group before an opponent lands on yours.

9. KNOW WHEN AND WHERE TO BUILD HOUSES AND HOTELS

Building advances your ability to bankrupt your opponents. Many players build all they can afford. Often, however, this strategy results in losses when houses must be torn down to pay rents or other penalties.

You *should* build when you form the first monopoly.

You *should* build when you can do so and still be left with enough cash to pay a "high probability" expense — namely, rents on Railroads or Utilities, Luxury Tax, and the "nasty" unexposed Community Chest or Chance cards. $150 to $200 is all the cash you need to hold onto if there are no other monopolies against you. $300 to $400 in cash is recommended if there are one or more monopolies developed against you.

You *should* build late in the game, in "all or nothing" situations if you think you can financially cripple an opponent by doing so.

When you build, build according to these principles:

Build a monopoly up to at least three houses per property before you start building on a second monopoly. (Note that rents rise dramatically once a third house is added to a property.)

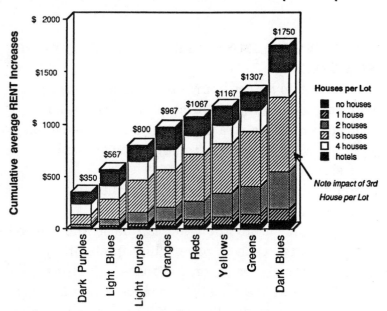

How each row of Houses increases av. RENT per Group

If you can afford an extra house, put it on the most expensive property of the monopoly.

Build up to the fourth house or hotel level only if you have plenty of cash to spare, unless the group is one of the first three on the board (Dark Purple, Light Blue, Light Purple). Due to the low rents of these groups, you *should* try to build hotels here.

Early in the game, develop a low-rent monopoly as soon as you can in an attempt to bankrupt your opponents before "heavier" monopolies are developed against you.

When buying a second extra house for a three-property group, put it on the middle property if the group is Light Blue or Orange. Put the house on the first property if the group is Light Purple, Red, Yellow, or Green.

10. KNOW WHEN TO CAUSE A BUILDING SHORTAGE

If you have only low-rent monopolies, quickly build three or four houses per property to restrict the availability of houses to owners of high-rent monopolies.

Never move up to a hotel *anywhere* if the return of houses to the bank would enable an opponent to develop an expensive monopoly. (Example: the Yellow monopoly has just been formed. There are only three houses in the bank, but six hotels. You own the light blues with four houses each. *Do not* buy hotels. Doing so would give the player owning the Yellows an opportunity to build up to hotels on them.)

11. KNOW HOW TO GET THE MOST OUT OF MORTGAGING

Mortgaging is essential to raise money at crucial

moments in the game. Follow these guidelines when it comes time to mortgage.

Mortgage single properties first. Try not to mortgage a property from a group where you own two or more properties unless you absolutely have to. (You can't build on a color group you own if one of its properties is mortgaged!)

Mortgage single properties to raise cash if it helps you develop a monopoly up to at least three houses per property, (or hotels on the Light Blues or either Purple group).

When you must decide between mortgaging properties, use this list to prioritize.

Try to mortgage:

1st. Colored properties closest to GO.

2nd. A Single Utility.

3rd. Railroads.

4th. The Utility monopoly.

Utilities produce a lot of cash, and you will need cash to unmortgage properties!)

Bear in mind, though, that Illinois, New York, and Boardwalk have higher chances of getting landed on than many of the other properties, with Illinois the highest. Don't mortgage these properties if you can avoid it.

If your opponents develop more expensive monopolies, resist the temptation to mortgage heavily to develop a lower-rent monopoly to your limit, unless you're in an "all-or-nothing" situation late in the game.

Pay off mortgages only if you have developed your

monopolies to at least three houses per property and can afford to unmortgage.

When paying off mortgages, pay them off in the reverse order in which you mortgaged them, *unless* you can develop a new unmortgaged monopoly by doing otherwise.

12. KNOW HOW TO TRADE

To make beneficial trades, you need to be familiar with some basic principles.

Early in the game, for instance, trade to get low-cost, steady income producing properties: namely, the Railroads or Utilities! (Railroads are preferable over Utilities.)

Try to trade for a monopoly that can "dominate" quickly (see the Tip Sheets).

To get such a monopoly, your best trading material might include the Railroads, the Utilities, or the Dark Purple monopoly, as well as single properties that do not yield an opponent a more dominant monopoly.

When trading developable properties, try to trade for properties of equal or greater value and those that lie closer to Free Parking.

Parker Brothers prints about 50 billion dollars worth of MONOPOLY money in one year.

Use the Property Tip Sheets to determine which color groups to trade for, based on what you can afford to develop, and which groups have a better chance of redeeming your investment.

If you end up with a monopoly whose dominance comes later in the game, don't overextend yourself. The lower-rent monopolies are likely to give you trouble if you deplete your cash too early. Be patient until your assets grow.

Trade for cash only if your "gain" is likely to be more than your opponent's. This means that he or she shouldn't be able to afford to develop a powerful monopoly as a result of the trade. You, on the other hand, should be in a position to put the cash to good advantage — by building further or bolstering your cash reserves.

Use common sense. Make a trade only if you're sure it will improve your chances of winning. Don't allow another player to persuade you to trade just for the sake of trading.

When you interest an opponent in a trade, try to let your adversary do most of the suggesting. You may get more than you thought you could. (Nevertheless, if you feel you can show your opponent why a particular trade is worthwhile for both of you, don't hesitate to demonstrate why.) Try to show your opponent why his or her demands are too high if you are unwilling to pay his price.

13. KNOW HOW TO CONDUCT YOURSELF AS A PLAYER

This is the most important principle of all!

Present yourself as the type of player others won't mind losing to.

Most players don't like losing to:

-browbeaters
-insulters
-know-it-alls
-careless players

-inconsiderate players

Most players don't mind losing to opponents who are:

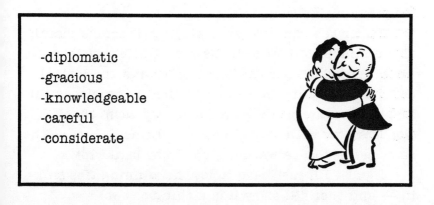

-diplomatic
-gracious
-knowledgeable
-careful
-considerate

Why is this so important? MONOPOLY usually cannot be won without gaining the cooperation of players in trades and financial settlements. If you don't have a reasonable rapport with your opponents, you'll have a tough time making beneficial trades.

"That's quite a list," I remarked.

"It becomes quite instinctive after you use it for several games," Pennybags responded. "Naturally, there are other subtleties players will uncover in time — but I've never liked over-burdening anyone with minutia. You pick up the finer points through play, by applying the main principles. For example, if you know the real value of a property group, you can sense the ramifications of a trade that produces new monopolies. Since luck plays such an important role in the game, players must maintain flexibility, without being locked into too many rigid formulas."

As for the game we were playing, it served mainly as a reminder of how well the Rich Uncle's system can work. Pennybags got the Light Blues and the Reds. I got the Light Purples. In rapid order, he developed the Light Blues, drained a good deal of my cash, then clobbered me with three houses on Illinois. Just as the game seemed to be warming up, I was bankrupt.

I guess I'll just have to let the winning tips sink in — and then I'll show him a thing or two!

FIVE
A MONOPOLY
PARTY — AND
SOME NEW WAYS
TO PLAY

MONOPOLY PARTY!

Pennybags' home really came to life that evening — eleven guests arrived, via special invitation, to compete in a MONOPOLY "mini-tournament." Madge told me she loved gatherings and had created a "winning formula" to make the dinner party a big hit, using MONOPOLY as its central theme.

The prior week, she'd mailed special invitations to each guest. (She was good enough to give me one to reproduce in this book. You can copy it for use with your own MONOPOLY party!)

Pennybags told me how the evening would go.

"Madge is quite a cook," he said. "She's created some great food, all inspired by MONOPOLY and Atlantic City. After dinner, our guests will each play two time-limit MONOPOLY games. Those players with the highest asset total will take home the door prizes. We've set-up three tables. At each table four players will compete. You'll be one of course."

"Of course."

"Now, to get things going quickly, I've devised a technique to get all the Title Deeds and a related amount of cash into circulation the moment the game begins."

Here's how he did it.

Pennybags had taken four envelopes and sorted the 28 Title Deeds into four sets. Each set was roughly equal in "value" — or relative worth after consulting each property's "payoff value" according to the Tip Sheets. Then he added some cash to each set, just enough so the actual value of the properties and the cash totaled close to $2200 per player.

"What I tried to do," Pennybags explained, "is set up each game as if it had been going long enough for each player to have completed three circuits around the board — and long enough for all the properties to have been purchased. To keep things fair, of course, I had to assure that the property holdings were roughly equal in strength."

Who gets what
at a MONOPOLY party...

Envelope #1: Baltic, Mediterranean, Kentucky, Indiana, Pacific, North Carolina, Pennsylvania, and $720 cash.

Envelope #2: Oriental, Vermont, Connecticut, Illinois, Boardwalk, Pennsylvania Railroad, B&O Railroad, and $840 cash.

Envelope #3: St. Charles, States, Virginia, New York, Park Place, Reading Railroad, Short Line, and $810 cash.

Envelope #4: St. James, Tennessee, Atlantic, Ventnor, Marvin Gardens, Electric Company, Water Works, and $740 cash.

These distributions give each competitor at least one complete monopoly, and encourage immediate trading. The ability to develop a powerful monopoly, as well, is roughly equal.

The guests had arrived.

After each player had been seated, the dice were passed around the table. The high thrower picked an envelope, opened it, and sorted the properties and cash. In turn, the table's remaining players did likewise. The game was now ready to begin.

A sixty-minute time limit was imposed — otherwise the rules were identical to those used in standard MONOPOLY. When time expired, each player totaled his assets and Pennybags recorded each total on a master scoresheet.

Next, each couple moved to the seats Pennybags had designated for Game Two. Again, the properties and cash were sealed in envelopes and passed out as before. After sixty minutes, the games were stopped and assets totaled. After a short break for refreshments, Pennybags announced the four highest asset totals and awarded the prizes.

"As you can imagine, this concept works great for four, eight, or as many as twelve players," Pennybags told me afterwards.

The games were fast-paced and exciting. My partner was a nephew of the Rich Uncle — Andy Pennybags. As I eventually learned, Andy was one of three identical triplets at the party, each bespectacled, each an aggressive MONOPOLY player, and each anxious to be just like their uncle when they grew up — rich! Andy played well, and we came in third out of the six couples. Not bad, I thought.

I did have a lot of fun — and Madge's treats were great!

MADGE PENNYBAGS' MONOPOLY PARTY RECIPIES
The Appetizers

Lucky Dice Canapes

Use thick, textured white bread. Trim crust, cut each slice into 4 squares. Spread with a mixture of 1/2 cup cream cheese, 2 teaspoons cream, 1 tablespoon anchovy paste, plus a small minced onion, salt and pepper to taste. Decorate each square with capers arranged to look like sides on the dice — from 1 to 6 capers per square.

$1 White Cucumber and Cream Dip

Grate 1/2 cucumber peeled and seeded, add 1 cup of sour cream, 1/4 teaspoon each of salt and white pepper. Mix thoroughly, then top with additional cucumber gratings.

$5 Pink Shrimp Dip

Blend in a food processor: 1/2 small can of salad shrimp, 1/4 cup of sour cream, 2 tablespoons of cream, a few grinds of fresh pepper, 1 small onion, 1 tablespoon of ketchup. Add the remaining 1/2 can of shrimp and mix thoroughly. Save a few shrimp for garnish.

$10 Yellow Curry and Carrot Dip

Mix well: 1/2 cup mayonnaise, 1 medium grated carrot, 1½ teaspoons curry powder. Garnish with additional carrot gratings.

$20 Green Avocado Dip

Blend in a food processor: 1/2 cup sour cream, 1 very ripe avocado, 1 minced scallion, 1/4 teaspoon chili powder. Garnish with a well-minced parsley leaf.

$50 Blue Cheese Dip

Combine 1/2 cup blue cheese dressing, 1/4 cup chopped black olives, 1/4 cup sour cream. You may add 2 drops of blue food coloring if desired. Top with 1/4 cup crumbled blue cheese.

The Main Course

Seashore Seafood Salad

3 cups dry seashell pasta — cook according to package directions. Chill. Cook 1 lb. small salad shrimp for 2½ minutes in boiling water. Chill.

Charles Darrow may be known as the "father of MONOPOLY," but Parker Brothers' Robert Barton was perhaps more instrumental in ensuring the game's success. Barton came to terms not only with Knapp Electric, which brought out two "precursor" games, but also with Elizabeth Magie-Phillips, inventor of THE LANDLORD'S GAME.

Dressing

2/3 cup olive oil

1/3 cup red wine vinegar

1 tablespoon Dijon mustard

1½ tablespoons Parmesan cheese

1 tablespoon freshly chopped parsley

1/2 teaspoon Mrs. Dash herb mix

1/2 teaspoon (10 or 12 grinds) black pepper

1/4 teaspoon salt (or to taste)

Mix dressing ingredients in medium size bowl with whisk or electric mixer until thick and creamy looking, (1-2 minutes). Pour over chilled shrimp and pasta shells. Then add 1/2 cup cooked broccoli florettes, 2 large scallions chopped fine, 1/2 cup red roasted Italian peppers (available in jars), and 1/2 cup black olives. Mix all ingredients together and chill until served.

Marinated MONOPOLY Mignon

Preheat oven to 450 degrees.

Prepare 4 lb. tenderloin by trimming fat and any visible tendons. Rub well with olive oil and 1 large minced or pressed garlic clove. Sprinkle generously with black pepper. Refrigerate for at least 1/2 hour. Do not add salt as this dries out the roast. Cook for 30 minutes for rare, 40 minutes for medium, or 50 minutes for well done. (Cook in same pan as potatoes, below.)

PARK PLACE Potatoes

Preheat oven to 450 degrees.

Peel 8 large potatoes, rub with olive oil and sprinkle

with onion powder. Line roasting pan with foil, coat
with olive oil. Arrange potatoes around edges of pan,
allowing room for roast to be added during baking.
Bake potatoes for 1 hour.

TENNESSEE AVENUE Tomatoes

Preheat oven to 450 degrees.
Slice 1/4" off tops of 8 medium-sized ripe tomatos. Top
with plain bread crumbs, 2 tablespoons per tomato.
Sprinkle each with a pinch of basil and small pinch of
mint. Top with a small pat of butter. Place in foil-lined
pan and add to oven during the final 30 minutes of
baking.

Millionaire's Mushroom Sauce

Saute in 1 tablespoon of butter and 1 tablespoon of
olive oil, 1 small sliced onion and 1 cup sliced
mushrooms on medium high heat in frying pan until
brown (4-5 minutes). Mix together 1 cup water, 1/2 cup
white wine or dry vermouth, 1 teaspoon Worcestershire
sauce, 1 tablespoon soy sauce, 1½ teaspoons of corn
starch. Add to pan with mushrooms and onions. Cook
until hot and bubbling (2-3 minutes). Serve with
MONOPOLY Mignon.

Though Charles Darrow retained
MONOPOLY's use of Atlantic City
street names, he himself was from
Germantown, Pennsylvania.

The Dessert

Beauty Contest Banana Yogurt Torte

Preheat oven to 325 degrees.

Put 1/2 lb. soft butter, 1⅔ cups sugar and 5 eggs into food processor. Process until smooth. Add 2 ripe bananas and 8 oz. of banana yogurt. Process again until smooth. Add 2 cups cake flour and 1/4 teaspoon salt. Process one more time until well mixed.

Pour into 9″ springform pan, well buttered and floured. Bake for 1 hour (or until toothpick in center of cake emerges clean). Top may split. Cool for one hour and then invert onto cake plate.

Glaze — To one cup of confectioner's sugar, add water, 1 tablespoon at a time (3-4 maximum), until the glaze mixture becomes a thick liquid. Pour over cake, allowing glaze to drip decoratively over the sides. Garnish with sliced bananas brushed with lemon juice to prevent browning.

Ever wonder exactly how much MONOPOLY money comes with a standard set? The total is $15,140.

An INVITATION
to PLAY a special party version of
the World's Most Popular Board Game
MONOPOLY

where: _____

_____

when: _____phone _____

Following a very special MONOPOLY dinner,
two 60 minute time-limit games will be played
with splendid prizes awarded to our winners.
A great time is guaranteed! **RSVP**

A CHANGE OF PACE

"Now, I don't want you to get me wrong," I told Pennybags after the guests left. "I like the party version of MONOPOLY. But I've got another suggestion for you."

"What's that?"

"How about saying something about the other popular variations of MONOPOLY? I know you like to play by the book, but everyone knows that MONOPOLY is great for socializing. Perhaps some of the legendary house rules and game variations suit that purpose just fine as well!"

"Well, I'm a stickler for the rules..."

"I know."

"But I can't see any harm in describing a few new twists you can add to the game — just for variety's sake."

VARIATIONS ON THE RULES THAT YOU CAN USE IN STANDARD PLAY

1. Prohibit players who are in Jail from collecting rents, building houses or hotels, mortgaging properties or engaging in trading activities.

2. Make Free Parking a bonus space. At the start of play place a $500 bill under this corner of the board. All money due the Bank for fines, taxes, or building repairs goes under Free Parking (but not money from the purchase of Title Deeds, buildings, or rents and mortgage revenue). Whenever a player lands on Free Parking, that player collects the entire sum currently lying there. (The initial $500 is not replaced once claimed. It is just a bonus for the lucky first player.) This is a rule that makes for *long* games.

3. Do not allow any player to buy property during his or her first trip around the board. (This rule variation tends to balance out the disadvantage experienced by those moving last in a game involving five or more players.)

4. Pay $400 rather than the normal $200 for landing on GO.

5. Allow immunity to be granted as part of a trade. Let's say you trade a property to an opponent who gains a monopoly. As part of the trade, that player grants you one or more "free passes" in the event of your landing on the property you traded to him (or, perhaps, any property in the monopoly).

6. Establish new rules with regard to loans. For example, when you form a monopoly, feel free to take a loan from the Bank equal to the color group's printed cumulative value. (A loan on the Light Blue monopoly would gain you $320.) Use the money you borrow as you see fit. Signify you've taken a loan by placing colored edges of the title deeds of the monopoly under the board before you, face up. Unlike mortgaged properties, *these properties remain active.* What's the catch? The next time a double-six is rolled, the bank calls in *all* outstanding loans. Each player must pay

MONOPOLY is marketed in 33 countries — and printed in many languages, including English (with separate editions for America and the United Kingdom), French, Italian, Greek, Norwegian, Portuguese, Japanese, Spanish, Catalan, German, Flemish, Dutch, Swedish, Finnish, and Indian.

back his loans at face value plus 10% (on the Light Blue monopoly, $352 would be repaid). If the loan cannot be repaid, the Bank must seize the monopoly and immediately auction it off, as a monopoly, to the highest bidder. (Naturally, all buildings on the monopoly must be sold back to the Bank prior to auctioning.)

7. Use quick auctions as a way to get all properties into play in a reasonable time. Whenever a doubles is thrown, the next unowned property clockwise from GO should be auctioned off by the banker, after the player throwing doubles completes his or her move.

8. Allow Chance and Community Chest Cards to be sold, before drawn, by the player who lands on the space. The seller collects the agreed-upon price, then the purchaser draws the card and follows its instructions. Play then proceeds in normal fashion — with the player to the seller's left rolling next.

"CLOCKWATCHER" GAME VARIATIONS — FOR THOSE IN A HURRY!

Time Limit MONOPOLY:

Before starting play, simply agree on an ending time. In Tournament play, this variation is used exclusively in the preliminary rounds — 90 minutes is the preset time limit. At the conclusion of play, the banker halts play and each player totals the value of his assets, according to their printed values. The player with highest asset total wins.

Short Game **MONOPOLY:**

The Banker shuffles all the Title Deeds and deals two to each player before sorting the deck in preparation for play. Each player pays for the deeds he or she receives. Hotels can be built after the *third* house is erected on each lot of a color-group (rather than the fourth.) Rents remain the same. If hotels are broken down, they are worth four houses in value (not five). The game ends when the *second* player has gone bankrupt. If the second player to go bankrupt has gone bankrupt to another player, he or she must, of course, hand over all assets to the collecting player. The game is over; the remaining players then total assets. The player with highest asset total wins.

SIX
TOURNAMENT
MONOPOLY — AND
HOW YOU CAN
PLAY IT

MONOPOLY FOR KEEPS

"MONOPOLY can be played on two levels," Pennybags reminded me. "It can be played merely for enjoyable social interaction, or in the spirit of pure competition. Now, for someone who wants to compete *and* become the best player he or she can be, there is the high-charged world of MONOPOLY Tournaments.

"A new United States Champion is crowned every three years; the following year a new World Champion emerges from a field of twenty or more national champs, including the U.S. champ. The World Tournaments have been held in cities like Monte Carlo and Palm Beach, not to mention right here in Atlantic City."

Pennybags proceeded to give me all the details.

LOCAL TOURNAMENTS

Soon after each World Championship is completed, Parker Brothers officials begin to assist organizations around the country to hold local MONOPOLY tournaments — the first step towards crowning the next United States champion.

Groups like the Boy and Girl Scouts, the Department of Public Works, or the local Chamber of Commerce will sponsor these tournaments. Notices appear in local newspapers to invite anyone interested.

On the day of the tournament, players gather and are briefed on all procedures and rule clarifications. Players are conditioned from the beginning to play in the same uniform manner that is standard in both the

U.S. and World Championship tournaments.

There are some important differences from the "orthodox" rules. Players usually play three games, each of which is limited to ninety minutes in length. At the conclusion of each game, the tournament officials tally the asset value accumulated by each player. At the end of all three rounds, the six players with the highest asset totals compete to determine the local champion.

THE STATE CHAMPION

When all the local tournaments are completed, the asset totals of all local champs are compared. The local champ with the highest asset value is crowned the state's champion by Parker Brothers officials.

FINANCE and FORTUNE, two "precursor" games, were eventually published by Parker Brothers — though both were substantially modified to clearly separate them from the Rich Uncle's game. FORTUNE did not succeed, but FINANCE was published well into the 1970's.

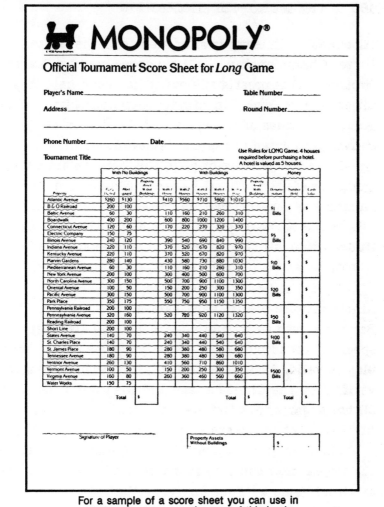

MONOPOLY®

Official Tournament Score Sheet for *Long* Game

Player's Name _____   Table Number _____

Address _____   Round Number _____

_____

Phone Number _____ Date _____

Tournament Title _____

Use Rules for LONG Game. 4 houses required before purchasing a hotel. A hotel is valued as 5 houses.

Property	With No Buildings			With Buildings						Money		
	Cost Listed	Most Used	Property Assets W/out Buildings	With 1 House	With 2 Houses	With 3 Houses	With 4 Houses	With Hotel	Property Assets With Buildings	Denomination	Number Held	Cash Value
Atlantic Avenue	$260	$130		$410	$560	$710	$860	$1010				
B & O Railroad	200	100								$1 Bills	$	$
Baltic Avenue	60	30		110	160	210	260	310				
Boardwalk	400	200		600	800	1000	1200	1400				
Connecticut Avenue	120	60		170	220	270	320	370				
Electric Company	150	75								$5 Bills	$	$
Illinois Avenue	240	120		390	540	690	840	990				
Indiana Avenue	220	110		370	520	670	820	970				
Kentucky Avenue	220	110		370	520	670	820	970				
Marvin Gardens	280	140		430	580	730	880	1030		$10 Bills	$	$
Mediterranean Avenue	60	30		110	160	210	260	310				
New York Avenue	200	100		300	400	500	600	700				
North Carolina Avenue	300	150		500	700	900	1100	1300				
Oriental Avenue	100	50		150	200	250	300	350		$20 Bills	$	$
Pacific Avenue	300	150		500	700	900	1100	1300				
Park Place	350	175		550	750	950	1150	1350				
Pennsylvania Railroad	200	100										
Pennsylvania Avenue	320	160		520	720	920	1120	1320		$50 Bills	$	$
Reading Railroad	200	100										
Short Line	200	100										
States Avenue	140	70		240	340	440	540	640		$100 Bills	$	$
St. Charles Place	140	70		240	340	440	540	640				
St. James Place	180	90		280	380	480	580	680				
Tennessee Avenue	180	90		280	380	480	580	680				
Ventnor Avenue	260	130		410	560	710	860	1010				
Vermont Avenue	100	50		150	200	250	300	350		$500 Bills	$	$
Virginia Avenue	160	80		260	360	460	560	660				
Water Works	150	75										
			Total $						Total $			Total $

_____
Signature of Player

Property Assets Without Buildings $ ____ . ____

For a sample of a score sheet you can use in your own games, see the rear of this book.

THE UNITED STATES CHAMPIONSHIP

Approximately a year after the first local tournament is held, the process is completed and all state champions are determined. Champions are declared in all fifty states, as well as Washington, DC and Puerto

Rico. Each winner is invited to attend the United States Championship — all expenses paid by Parker Brothers. This prestigious event has been held in such cities as New York, Washington, Atlantic City, and Los Angeles. Hordes of reporters and TV cameramen converge to cover the multi-day event.

Prior to the start of play, the Tournament's Chief Judge briefs the official Bankers. (These men and women are usually *real-life* bankers from the city where the tournament is being held.) Then the Chief Judge briefs all the contestants, and answers all questions about procedures and rules interpretations.

As in the local tournaments, a series of three ninety-minute preliminary games are played. A Chief Banker serves as official timekeeper. He also dispenses specially coded money to visually assure that money in play is valid. Assets are tallied after each game and verified by the Chief Banker and his committee. When all three games are finished, the four players with the highest asset totals are announced as the Finalists.

The four Finalists, and the reigning United States Champion, now compete in a five player, winner-take-all, final game *without* any time limit.

When the excitement-packed final game is over, a new United States Champion emerges victorious!

The U.S. champ is invited to attend the World Championship, held the following year.

MONOPOLY®

Parker Brothers Real Estate Trading Game

TOURNAMENT POINTS TO REMEMBER

1. To raise money to pay *debts,* only houses and hotels can be sold back to the bank (at half price), never properties. If a debt is owed to another player, properties may be sold to a third player only if sufficient money is raised to cover the debt. If not, the properties are turned over *as is* (and not mortgaged if unmortgaged at the time the debt is incurred.)

2. The owner may not collect his *rents* if he fails to ask for it before the second player following throws the dice. This means: Player A lands on your property. Player B has his turn. You must collect your rent before Player C throws the dice.

3. If you throw a doubles to get out of Jail, you move forward that number of spaces as your turn. You do not throw again. However, if you pay to get out of Jail prior to rolling, and you throw doubles, you may throw again as usual.

4. Though you need not disclose how much *money* you have, you must keep your money on the table in plain view at all times.

5. All trades are based on assets owned at the time of the trade. No options or immunity from paying future rents may be granted, nor may partnerships be formed.

6. Trading is permitted during a player's turn or in between other players' turns, but not during an opposing player's turn.

7. Players cannot sell *Chance* or *Community Chest* cards prior to revealing them to other players.

8. Players may *not* consult or seek advice from friends or game observers while the game is in progress.

9. *Tokens* used in Tournament play *must* be from the game itself.

10. While a *Building Shortage* exists, players desiring to buy the houses remaining in the bank have priority over those wishing to break down hotels.

11. In *Preliminary Games,* when only *two* players remain, no further trades or deals are permitted.

THE WORLD MONOPOLY CHAMPIONSHIP

National champions from all over the world send their winners to attend the World Tournament. (Players from foreign countries compete in a manner similar to that of the U.S. to determine their national champion, as supervised by official MONOPOLY licensee companies in those nations.) The World Tournament is usually held in the United States because most national champions wish to make a trip to the birthplace of MONOPOLY.

Given the role of luck in MONOPOLY, each game seems to defy conventional handicapping. Instead of predictably narrowing down the field, the championships tend to have more than their share of rollercoaster rides of uncertainty and suspense.

At the start of the tournament, the Chief Judge briefs the bankers and the contestants. Again, three 90-minute preliminary games are played. Assets are tallied and the four players with the highest totals will compete, along with the current world champ, in the final game.

Played without any time limit, the final game is both an intense game and media experience. Within a gaily decorated ballroom, reporters crowd to see the proceedings. Seated at the table are the five finalists, the Chief Judge and Chief Banker. Slightly behind some of the players are official interpreters for foreign competitors.

Television lights illuminate the scene, cameras quietly whirl and the game begins. Before the final game begins, players roll to see which player has first choice of playing token. Then, each rolls one more time to determine sequence of play.

During play, the Chief Banker handles all transactions with the bank, while the Chief Judge answers all questions and resolves any disputes promptly. Usually, the Chief Judge is also fitted with a microphone, so the crowd can hear the progress of the game as they watch it on the large television monitors.

The game soon builds in intensity. These are the best players in the world and the quality of the game usually reflects this fact. Key trades are made, monopolies are formed. Buildings rise. With surprising rapidity, one player goes bankrupt; then another; then another.

Finally, the last two players lock heads in a battle to the finish. The press jostles for position. The crowd reacts audibly whenever one of the final players is granted a stay in Jail, winning a temporary reprieve from an opponent's monopolies. Groans — or cheers —

Can you name this character?

(It's Vern Verity, the IRS officer!)

are heard whenever a big rent comes due. Each player stretches resources to the limit. The maximum number of buildings are on the board. It's "crunch time."

Suddenly, one player breathes a sigh of relief — the crowd gasps. The opposing player has landed on a powerhouse monopoly and can't meet the rent. The player tears down hotels and houses, mortgages property, and watches victory slowly slipping away.

The dice tumble for the last few times. The player on the ropes lands once more on a devastating monopoly. This time it is over. Handshakes are exchanged as the Chief Judge hurries to place the champion's sash over the winner's shoulder before the press engulfs the new champ.

Minutes later, at the main podium, the finalists are honored, and given their prizes. Then the big winner is presentĕd, handed the MONOPOLY plaque commemorating a great win, and awarded the grand prize — which in past championships have included a MONOPOLY game filled with *real* cash, a $10,000 shopping spree, or a fabulous all-expenses-paid vacation to an exotic locale.

The Champion is now surrounded by television cameras, interviewed in rapid-fire fashion by well-known reporters and celebrities. By the next day, he or she is seen all over America on programs like "Today" and "Good Morning America," as well as network evening news programs. And since many of the world champions have come from other countries, the news spreads internationally just as quickly.

HIGHLIGHTS FROM TOURNAMENT PLAY

1979 United States Championship

The reigning U.S. Champion was Dana Terman, a twenty-four year old Maryland native and salesman for an auto dealership. Terman developed a reputation as a tough and wily player who knew the game inside and out. In the finals, his most formidable competitor — and the favorite of both the crowd and media — was an unflappable ten-year old named Angelo Repole from Staten Island. Repole had already beaten many seasoned competitors — all over thirty — in his prior matches. By the time the U.S. Championship rolled around, the press was calling Repole the "MONOPOLY Whiz Kid."

One of Terman's advantages was the fact that he'd attended each of the four regional tournaments. (State champions competed in "regionals" back in 1979.) As a result, he had the line on his opponents. He knew Repole was the most resolute of the bunch, the only one with the necessary killer instinct to wipe out any opponent on the ropes. While Repole had never seen

Each year, the makers of MONOPOLY produce more than twice as much play money as the U.S. Mint does actual money!

Terman in action, he had heard of Dana's remarkable comebacks in the prior world tournament. Terman was a consummate MONOPOLY player and probably knew the game better than any prior U. S. champ.

While Repole was certainly both cute and outspoken, he was also a marvelous player who had had only six months of playing experience prior to the tournament! He had grown-up street-smart — he knew not to back down to any player, even one several times his age, and he was not intimidated during the crucial deal-making moments of the game. In fact, through the use of exceptional hard-line tactics, he usually took charge in trading sessions!

In his regional victory, good luck had also helped Angelo. He landed on all three light purple properties in successive trips around the board. He exploited this "natural monopoly" quickly and decisively.

In the U.S. Championship, Angelo found his luck mirroring his earlier experience. He got the Light Purple monopoly early, and the field narrowed quickly. It was a two-man game — Terman and Repole.

While Dana had used all of his savvy to stay in the game, he now found himself with a lot of properties but very little cash. His only hope lay with the Dark Blue monopoly — a red hotel standing dramatically on Boardwalk and four houses crowding Park Place.

Angelo's luck held firm in the endgame. For what seemed like the tenth time, he skipped past Boardwalk, landing on GO. Dana was not as lucky. States Avenue and its hotel greeted him with a $750 rent. Angelo cheered reflexively. Most of Dana's undeveloped properties were flipped white-side up. Only mortgage money was keeping him alive.

Angelo, for his part, remained fortunate. He landed in Jail, avoiding the worst of Terman's traps. The bubble gum in his mouth popped faster now; he looked forward to a long stay while Dana remained exposed, dancing towards the minefields located on St. Charles, States, and Virginia Avenues.

But on his very first turn in Jail, Angelo threw double-sixes, and was forced from the safety of his cell. (The odds of throwing two 6's are 1 in 36.) Twelve spaces later Angelo touched down on the red question mark separating Kentucky from Indiana Avenue.

Even before Angelo drew the card, Terman knew who had won. Observant spectators noticed a slight grin forming on Terman's lips.

Previously, fifteen Chance cards had been drawn. Only one of the sixteen remained unseen. (The odds of any one card being the sixteenth drawn are 1 out of 16.)

Angelo flipped over the card.

It read: Advance Token to Boardwalk.

Call it a 576-to-1 shot. Repole had some rent to pay.

Terman, suddenly, was solvent again. He unmortgaged the Yellows and built houses on that monopoly — and the Reds as well.

In no time, Angelo was outgunned. Dana Terman accepted the ten-year-old's brave handshake and remained U.S. champion.

1983 World Championship

In 1983, the World Championship took place by the sea in Palm Beach, Florida at the venerable Breakers Hotel.

This tournament featured another youngster — fourteen-year-old James Mallet of the United Kingdom, who willingly offered his winning advice to the press, and whose skill catapulted him into the final round. There he faced four older players including the champs from Peru, Venezuela, Austria and Australia (who climbed from ninth place to fourth in the final round and squeaked into the final game).

Mallet did well early on, repeating history by landing on all three Light Purples and claiming the monopoly. But after two of his opponents went bankrupt, he was confronted by a formidable array of houses on Boardwalk and Park Place, which soon made him the latest victim of methodical Greg Jacobs of Australia.

Jacobs, an extremely likeable man, had used artful reasoning to keep his opponents from making damaging deals. Soon, the final opponent bowed to the Aussie's four-monopoly stranglehold on the board. (1983 was a

The longest MONOPLY game played on the back of a firetruck lasted 101 hours.

banner year for Australia in many arenas, including MONOPOLY!)

Jacobs' victory, smooth and well-played, was largely due to his instinctive knowledge of the value of each color group. He had been playing MONOPOLY since he was *five!*

The day following his victory, he was entitled to spend his winnings — $10,000 — in a four-hour shopping spree on prestigious Worth Avenue.

What would he buy? the press wondered. Imported Italian shoes? Gold jewelry? Diamonds?

Jacobs calmly purchased a scarf for his wife and a few toys for his kids. Then he walked into a broker's office and plunked the remainder of the money — $9700 — into precious metals and stocks. (Incidentally, the stock he purchased tripled in the next three years.)

What's that? You were wondering what Jacobs does for a living? He's a real estate agent, of course.

1985 United States Championship

The next United States Championship took place in Union Station, Los Angeles. There, a jovial bald-headed accountant from Florida named Jim Forbes claimed the title. The following September, Forbes arrived in Atlantic City to do battle with twenty foreign champions.

In a ballroom of the Claridge Casino, overlooking Park Place and the Boardwalk, the final game took place on a drizzly afternoon following a long bus ride from New York (where the preliminary games had been played).

Jason Bunn of England took the contest. Bunn was a test engineer from Leeds, England who practiced every lunch hour with his workmates — an intelligent and analytical bunch to say the least! Luck was with him as — like Angelo Repole and James Mallet before him — he again formed a natural monopoly on the Light Purples without having to make a trade. He gained a quick advantage over all four of his opponents and won handily. His last remaining opponent was defending champion Greg Jacobs, whose initial luck had been poor. Jacobs had been unable to acquire many good properties early in the game. Only through his skill and knowledge had he kept alive his hopes of repeating. In the end, however, the Englishman was too much for him.

Bunn stands ready to defend his crown in London in the fall of 1988.

THE HONOR ROLL OF MONOPOLY CHAMPIONS

Year	U.S. Representative	World Champion
1973	Lee Bayrd, Los Angeles, CA	Lee Bayrd
1974	Alvin Aldridge, Dayton OH	Alvin Aldridge
1975	Gus Gostomelsky, Skokie, IL	John Mair, Ireland
1977	Dana Terman, Wheaton, MD	Cheng Seng Kwa, Singapore
1980	Dana Terman	Cesare Bernabei, Italy
1983	Jerome Dausman, Washington, DC	Greg Jacobs, Australia
1985	William Forbes, Winter Haven, FL	Jason Bunn, U.K.
1988	Gary Peters, Hallandale, FL	?????????????

I was hypnotized by Pennybags' accounts of the tournaments.

"You don't suppose. . . that is, you don't think. . ."

"Speak up!" the Rich Uncle barked. "I don't suppose what? Your readers might actually *enter* a local tournament? Try to make it on to the finals?"

"Well, yes. . ."

There was a pause.

"I don't see why not. Here's who they should contact."

MONOPOLY Tournament Director
Parker Brothers
50 Dunham Road
Beverly MA 01915

SEVEN
IN THE WORDS OF
THE CHAMPIONS

THE EXPERTS SPEAK

Here, in their own words, is the advice several MONOPOLY champions have offered on high-level, high-stakes MONOPOLY.

Angelo Repole — 1979 Eastern Regional Champ; 2nd place finish in U.S. Championship at age 10.

Q. Can you outline your basic strategy?
A. "Buy every property you land on, but don't overextend yourself — especially when building. Hope that bad luck doesn't overpower your strategies."

Q. Do you get nervous when playing players older than yourself?
A. "No!"

Dana Terman — 1977 and 1979 U.S. Monopoly Champ at ages 22 and 24.

Q. What is your advice for winning the game?
A. "Know the rules inside and out, use them for maximum advantage. Always play to drive another player out of the game as quickly as possible."

Cesare Bernabei — Italian. 1980 World Champion at age 26.

Q. How do you win?
A. "I keep trying to get the best deal I can without giving away too much. Once you make a bad

trade you can't recover. I try to show the other guy why the trade I've proposed is good for him too."

Jerome Dausman — 1982 United States Champion at age 29.

Q. What advice do you have for the "amateur" MONOPOLY players out there?
A. "Play with good sportsmanship but also play smart. Know the rules and basic strategies and use them well."

James Mallet — 1983 United Kingdom Champion, 3rd place in 1983 World Championship at age 14.

Q. Does it bother you to play older players?
A. "It doesn't bother me to play older, more experienced players. You've just got to play the best game you can and hope the dice go your way. I won't tell you all my strategies, but I will tell you I like to play a 'housing shortage' strategy instead of building up to hotels. . . because it prevents your opponents from developing fully."

Q. What has MONOPOLY taught you?
A. "Well, I started playing when I was four or five. I learned to count on it, learned to read on it, and learned to lose on it. So it's helped me to grow up!"

Bill Forbes — 1984 U.S. Champion at age 34.

Q. What's your secret strategy?
A. "Buy *everything* unowned that you land on."

Q. Do you feel bad when you bankrupt an opponent?
A. "Not in the least!"

Tommy Glynn — 1985 Irish Champion at age 20.

Q. What do you find appealing about MONOPOLY?
A. "It has a strong human element when you're wheeling and dealing. It's like life itself."

Jason Bunn — 1985 United Kingdom and World Champion at age 25.

Q. Is MONOPOLY skill or luck?
A. "Fifty-fifty skill and luck. I equate [MONOPOLY] with a game of poker. You get cards — Title Deeds — as you go around the board. And you've got to play the cards you get to your advantage, just like in a game of poker."

If one or both dice roll off the board, or land on or lean against a card deck, the roll is invalid. Roll them again.

Gary Peters — 1987 United States Champion at age 42.

Q. Whom did you compete against in the U.S. Championship?

A. "I competed against all the state champions who ranged in age from fourteen to fifty-four."

Q. How tough was the final game?

A. "It was the toughest game I've ever played."

Q. What's your best tip to new players?

A. "Know the real value of each monopoly, their rates of return, their likelihood of being landed on. Make your decision accordingly."

EIGHT
MONOPOLY THEN & NOW: NEW GAMES, NEW FORMATS, TELEVISION

A LONG, LONG WAY FROM ENDING

"The game certainly has come a long way," I said to Pennybags as we sat together in his den. "It's hard to believe that the same idea that got Darrow his initial rejection letter from Parker Brothers is now the center of so much attention. A worldwide following! Tournaments! Huge prizes! International media coverage!"

"It is remarkable," said the Rich Uncle, pondering the large globe at the center of the room decorated in MONOPOLY's colors, with Atlantic City perhaps more prominently displayed than on the one I'd known in school.

I felt a certain pride, not only in the game, but also in Pennybags himself, who'd contributed so much to its success. "What a happy ending to the story of the world's most popular game!"

The old man suddenly sat bolt upright in his chair.

"Ending?" he demanded. "Exactly what do you mean by that?"

I'd obviously touched a nerve.

"MONOPOLY may have been around for over fifty years, young man," he went on, "but it's a long, long way from ending! Why, there are new ideas, new games, even video versions of MONOPOLY!"

"It took quite a while for MONOPOLY to give birth to another game," Pennybags explained as he took a handsome package from his shelf. "Now, in all modesty, I must admit to endorsing a game named after me — that was back in 1946. RICH UNCLE, it was called. It featured me quite prominently. Very attractive piece of work, as you might imagine. But as enjoyable a game as it was, it wasn't based on my favorite — MONOPOLY. This game, ADVANCE TO BOARDWALK, is."

"It's an easy game to set up and play. Basically, the players are locked in a battle to control the most powerful hotels as they rise along the Boardwalk. You'll notice that the stakes seem a little higher than the original game: the lots range in value from four to eight *million* dollars! And there's no limit to a hotel's 'height' — or value — in this game."

"ADVANCE TO BOARDWALK," he continued, "like its parent, is a fascinating combination of luck and strategy. Most of the skill involves carefully nurturing limited resources, and making the most of what you have."

The Rich Uncle peered at me from across the room, a twinkle in his eye. The board was before him, ready for play.

"Care for a game, young man?"

Amazing as it may seem, I held my ground against the master and won my very first game of ADVANCE TO BOARDWALK.

"Something wrong with these odd-colored dice," Pennybags muttered, surveying the damage on the board. "Either that or there was a misprint on that confounded Hurricane card that blew the top unit off my hotel. Definitely some structural problems with this edition. We'll have to inform Charles so he can improve the thing."

I was flabbergasted. "You don't mean to say that Charles Darrow invented *this* game as well?"

"Phillips," he said brusquely, reaching for the phone. "Pleasant fellow named Charles Phillips invented this game." He dialed a number on the high-cradled, gold-plated luxury model that sat atop his desk.

After Pennybags had scolded poor Phillips for designing a game that could actually be lost when played according to the rules, I had the chance to ask the inventor a few questions of my own. After all, if I couldn't actually talk to Charles Darrow himself, here was the next best thing!

Charles Phillips

Q. It must be quite exciting to be regarded as the man who followed in Darrow's footsteps. Where did you get

the idea of inventing a game specifically about the
Boardwalk in Atlantic City?

A. Well, I always look for ideas in things around me.
Anything can trigger ideas for a game. I try to see the
world through the eyes of a kid. Of course, I see most
things as a game anyway. As it happened, a game
company executive suggested to me that a game about
Atlantic City could be hot. You know, there's a lot of
action and excitement down there. So I took a ride to
the city, and ended up going for a walk along the
Boardwalk. While soaking up the salt air and the smell
of taffy, I suddenly realized all the building that was
going on — casinos and hotels going up one after
another. I thought: these gambling companies are
playing a game themselves! That was it — the idea hit
me for a hotel-competition game. I knew if I could couple the idea with the colorful nature of the Boardwalk,
it would be a great game.

Q. It came that fast?

A. Well, the basic idea did. You see, I try to think in

The largest indoor MONOPOLY game
ever played used a gameboard 122 feet
by 12 feet in size.

terms that everyone can relate to, so the basic idea was very general. At first I thought of a gambling game, but the more I thought about it the more I knew that I had to avoid anything that smacked of sophisticated gambling or finance. I wanted a game for the family, not just gamblers. I mean, they already had their games — in the casinos! That meant the execution of the idea would have to be quite different. Yet, the person who'd suggested the idea to me really wanted a basic gambling game. So I knew I wasn't going to satisfy him when I went back to New York that afternoon.

Q. How long did it take to work out the idea?

A. About two weeks. My first idea was a track game played along the boardwalk and the adjoining avenue. I think that's Pacific Avenue. But the game still needed a spark. And back in 1984, when all this was happening, new board games weren't selling very well, so I knew I had to go one better.

Q. So you dropped the idea for a game about gambling in Atlantic City?

A. That's right. Randy Barton — who was then the President of Parker Brothers — told me that he felt the game could work very well with MONOPOLY, and that I should bring it to his company. He convinced me that a fun game aimed at kids and adults, and not at gamblers, would be popular.

Q. How long have you been inventing games?

A. About twenty years now.

Q. And ADVANCE TO BOARDWALK was your first game with Parker Brothers?

A. The first important one. It's sold very well, and been published actively now since 1985.

Q. How about those "structural problems" Pennybags found?

A. That's puzzling. You know, I can't help wondering if the old man shouldn't stick to MONOPOLY!

"He said I should *what?*"

The Rich Uncle had been quite agitated since the end of my discussion with Phillips. I decided a quick change of subject would probably be in my best interest.

What do they call Boardwalk in...?

France: Rue de la Paix
Germany: Schlossalle
Holland: Kalverstrat
The United Kingdom: Mayfair

"Phillips mentioned a man named Randy Barton. Is it true that he's the one who acquired ADVANCE TO BOARDWALK?"

Randolph Barton

"Barton, yes, he's the one. He's since retired; he and I do a bit of yachting together. You know, his grandfather was George Parker, who pioneered MONOPOLY in its early days." Pennybags paced over to a framed portrait of Mr. Parker.

"What else has happened to the initial MONOPOLY idea?" I asked, hoping he'd finally sit down.

"I'll show you. Take a look at this," he said, producing another game box. The cover depicted a colorful Pennybags running away from the policeman I remembered from the Chance cards.

"It's called FREE PARKING," he said proudly.

The new game looked nothing like ADVANCE TO BOARDWALK. The object of the game, as I learned from examining the contents of the box, is to be the first to score 200 points under strict "time limits" imposed through the game's "parking meter" timekeepers, and enforced rigidly by Officer Jones. The policeman figures prominently in the game's strategy. Evade him successfully, and you rack up the points. Unleash him on your opponents, and your position improves.

"Best two out of three?" asked my companion.

FREE PARKING is really a card game with a great twist — the "time is ticking" principle of the parking meters. The game requires that you stay on your toes and make the best of what you get on short notice.

Unfortunately, Pennybags outfoxed me this time around, hitting the magic 200-point mark well ahead of me. I realized I'd probably been pushing my luck in facing him again.

"I suppose I should have quit while I was ahead," I said as Pennybags put FREE PARKING away. He nodded in agreement, smiling victoriously.

"With a little time, you should recover."

"Thanks anyway," I continued diplomatically, "for the introduction to MONOPOLY's latest faces!"

"You're certainly welcome, young man," he replied, "but it's not over yet!" He glanced at his watch. "As a matter of fact, we finished just in time." He picked up a remote control box; the television built into the wall awakened.

After more than fifty years, MONOPOLY has come to television. For the first time in the game's history, its excitement will be captured in a special game show adaptation of MONOPOLY, produced by King World — the same company behind such popular shows as WHEEL OF FORTUNE and JEOPARDY!

The rules will sound familiar to fans of the standard board game. Each contestant begins with $1500 cash. Players battle to win monopolies, build houses and hotels, and amass the highest cash totals — then try to win a bonus round. Enlarged versions of the regular Tokens move around a giant, illuminated MONOPOLY board. Money is tabulated electronically. Enlarged Title Deeds are retained by each player, and there are special Chance and Community Chest decks.

The prizes become more lucrative as the game progresses — finally, once the champion is determined, he or she can win as much as $25,000 in cash!

"It seems exciting," I said to Pennybags as he finished. "It should be even more interesting to see or play!"

"Watch for it yourself and see!"

"I particularly like the use of a large, illuminated gameboard. It certainly is amazing what they can do with electronics these days!"

"Right you are — and now you can have your own illuminated gameboard at home."

"How?"

"MONOPOLY has entered the computer age as well!" said Pennybags enthusiastically. Two new games now portray regular MONOPOLY in a video form. The first is a cartridge for the Sega® video game system, the second is a floppy disk for home computers, notably the Commodore® 64 and 128. The disk format is produced by Virgin® Software. They've been quite successful with their game in England; now it's finally coming to America."

"And these games play just like regular MONOPOLY?"

"Precisely. And both games offer the opportunity for plenty of practice, thanks to their 'computer-controlled' players. These enable you to play competitively even if another human isn't around! And by the way, if you know my winning tips, you can use them to advantage in these games just as you can with regular MONOPOLY."

I was impressed. "We've really covered MONOPOLY from A to Z. Is there anything else on the agenda?"

"There certainly is," he replied. "Feel like a little test?"

Longest game in a bathtub: 99 hours

Longest game underwater: 45 days

Longest game played upside-down:
36 hours

NINE
THE MONOPOLY
QUIZ

FINALS

"Well, it's time for your final exam," Pennybags
said cheerfully. His pint-sized terrier, Scotty, sat on his
lap as we sipped coffee in the little man's study. "I've
told you all I know about MONOPOLY. Now we'll see if
you pass the course."

"A final exam? Don't you think I've learned what
you've taught me?"

"Now, now. Maybe you have learned the basics, but
your readers may have missed a point or two. So here's
their chance to check on their own MONOPOLY IQ.
Might not hurt you to give it a try, either."

Scotty scurried away as Pennybags produced his
neatly typed quiz. "It's actually quite straight-forward.
There are twenty-five multiple choice questions. If you
get 18 to 22 right, you've passed and are on your way
to being a fine player. If you get 23 or more correct,
you've earned high honors and are ready to take on a
national champion."

"And if I get less than 18 right, am I to repeat the
course?"

"You go directly to Jail. You do not pass GO. You do
not collect $200."

"Fair enough."

Here is Pennybags' quiz.

PROFESSOR PENNYBAGS' FINAL MONOPOLY EXAM

1. How many HOUSES should there be in the game?
    a) 24
    b) 28
    c) 32
    d) 36

2. How many HOTELS?
    a) 10
    b) 12
    c) 14
    d) 16

3. A COMMUNITY CHEST Card will most likely:
    a) move you to another space
    b) cost you money (a penalty)
    c) give you money (a reward)

4. A CHANCE Card will most likely:
    a) move you to another space
    b) cost you money
    c) give you money

5. The number most frequently rolled on the two dice is:
    a) 6
    b) 7
    c) 8
    d) 9
    e) doubles

6. The two least likely numbers to roll are:
>   a) 2 and 12
>   b) 3 and 11
>   c) 4 and 10

7. How many rolls of the dice are normally required to make a complete circuit of the board?
>   a) 4
>   b) 5
>   c) 6
>   d) 7

8. You own Illinois Avenue. An opponent owns Indiana. You land on Kentucky. Should you buy it?
>   a) yes
>   b) no

9. An opponent owns States, Atlantic and Marvin Gardens. Another opponent owns St. Charles and Ventnor. You land on Virginia. Should you buy it?
>   a) definitely
>   b) only if you want to
>   c) no

10. An opponent owns both States and St. Charles. You land on Virginia. Should you buy it?
>   a) definitely
>   b) only if you want to
>   c) no

11. You complete your first circuit around the board and land on Income Tax. On your circuit you earn $350 from Chance and Community Chest cards and paid no penalties or rents. Should you pay 10% of your assets or a straight $200 tax?

> a) 10%
> b) $200

12. You go to Jail at a time when eight properties remain unsold. No monopolies are formed. Should you pay $50 and get out of Jail on your very next turn, or stay in and just roll?

> a) pay $50 then roll
> b) just roll

13. You go to Jail at a time when all properties are owned and two monopolies are owned by opponents. Do you pay $50 on your first turn in Jail or stay in and just roll?

> a) pay $50 then roll
> b) just roll

14. You acquire all the Light Blue properties and form the first monopoly in the game. You have $450 in cash. What is the minimum number of houses you should build per Light Blue property?

> a) none
> b) one
> c) two
> d) three

15. You have five houses built among the Orange properties and have just acquired the Yellow color-group. You have $450 you wish to spend for houses. How do you spend it?

> a) build four houses among the Orange properties
>
> b) build one house on each Yellow
>
> c) build one house on Marvin Gardens and one on each Orange

16. You have two houses built on each Red property. You can afford to buy just two more houses for this group. Where do you build them?

> a) one each on Illinois and Indiana
>
> b) one each on Indiana and Kentucky
>
> c) one each on Illinois and Kentucky

17. You have 2 houses built on each Orange property. You can afford to buy just two more houses for this group. Where do you build them?

> a) one each on New York and Tennessee
>
> b) one each on St. James and Tennessee
>
> c) one each on New York and St. James

18. You have three houses each on the Light Blues. You also have enough money to buy Hotels on each property. There are nine houses left in the Bank. One opponent owns the Yellows, the other owns the Greens. Both have decided not to buy houses at this time. What do you do?

> a) buy 3 additional houses
>
> b) buy 3 hotels

19. Without taking actual money needs into account, rank these properties in order of which should be mortgaged first, second, third, and fourth.

> a) Oriental (you also own Connecticut)
> b) New York (you own no other Orange property)
> c) St Charles (you own no other Light Purple)
> d) Water Works (you do not own the Electric Company)

20. You're a bright and respected player. You have encouraged an opponent to trade with you. It is early in the game and no monopolies are yet formed. After a proposed trade, you'll end up with the Light Purples and $900 in cash; your opponent will get the Greens and have $500. Do you accept the trade?

> a) yes
> b) no

21. Same trade — only this time it is later in the game and each player, yourself included, has one undeveloped monopoly. After the trade, you'll have the Light Purples and $1600; your opponent will get the Greens and have $1200. Do you make the trade?

> a) yes
> b) no

22. It is the middle of the game. A proposed trade will bring you the Greens and give your opponent the Reds. You'll have $1200 to spend on houses and he'll have $1350. Neither of you has another monopoly. Assuming you buy six houses and he buys nine, which player has the more dominant monopoly as a result of the trade?

> a) you with the Greens (so the trade is a good one)
> b) he with the Reds (so the trade is questionable)

23. Which of these properties is most likely to be landed on in a typical game?

> a) New York
> b) Illinois
> c) Boardwalk

24. Which of these monopolies is most likely to be landed on in a typical game?

> a) the Railroads
> b) the Dark Blues
> c) the Reds

25. Is it better to own the Oranges and 3 hotels, or the Yellows with 3 houses each?

> a) the Oranges with hotels
> b) the Yellows with 3 houses

ANSWERS

1. c (see page 46)
2. b (see page 46)
3. c (see page 127)
4. a (see page 127)
5. b (see page 128)
6. a (see page 128)
7. c (see page 129)
8. a (see page 129)
9. b (see page 129)
10. a (see page 129)
11. b (you also earned $200 for passing GO. 10% would be $205 — see pages 56 and 130)
12. a (see page 131)
13. b (see page 131)
14. c (see page 131)
15. a (see page 131)
16. c (see page 131)
17. a (see page 131)
18. a (see page 131)
19. c,d,a,b (see page 134)
20. a (see page 135)
21. b (see page 135)
22. b (see pages 30 and 45)
23. b (see page 134)
24. a (see page 134)
25. a (see pages 98 and 105)

TEN
RETURN TO
"THE WORLD'S
PLAYGROUND"

THE TRAIN RIDE

"All aboard!" cried the conductor. "All aboard for Atlantic City!"

The sultry afternoon weighed heavily on me as I made my way through the crowd to the waiting train. A strange mist permeated the air and I overheard a lady next to me exclaim, "Thank God for Atlantic City. I can't wait to be away from this infernal place!"

Where on earth was I?

I fixed my gaze upon the shiny green passenger cars of the Boardwalk Flyer and edged my way along the left side of the concrete platform towards it. The crowd swept me forward — and into — one of its waiting doors.

Breathless, I found a plush seat and sat down, loosened my tie and got out my handkerchief to mop my brow. I looked down at my clothes. Who dressed me? Where did I get this suit?

As I collected my thoughts, I also tried to remember exactly why it was so important that I catch this train. The heat bearing down on my brain clouded any answer.

I couldn't help but notice a sturdy policeman, handcuffed to a simian-looking character seated next to him. The policeman held a whistle between his teeth and pointed a threatening finger towards anyone who seemed ready to move past him. His nameplate read Edgar Mallory, Chief of Police, Atlantic City. "It's off to jail with him," the cop was saying to the people across the aisle. "He's Jake the Jailbird. Nasty type. Doesn't talk much, either. Behind bars is where he belongs. A home for life, eh Jake?"

The gaunt-faced man sitting next to him did not reply.

A businessman saw me staring at the odd pair.

"Never seen a convict before?" he asked. His face was quite familiar. I looked away, trying not to call attention to myself.

"Less than nine months to go until April 15th!" he crowed suddenly, jarring me in the ribs.

The trip was getting stranger by the minute.

"Verity is my name," he went on. "Vern Verity. I'm going to Marven Gardens. But it's spelled with an 'e' you know, not an 'i'. Most people think it's Mar-vin, not -ven."

"Where have I seen you before?" I asked.

"Income tax refunds. I work for your friendly IRS."

I suddenly remembered that he also worked for the Community Chest!

Just then, three little boys ran down the aisle playing and yelling. I recognized them: the Pennybags triplets — Randy, Sandy, and my old partner Andy!

Looking around me, I saw people taking seats up and down the car, with the temperature and humidity common topics of discussion. Across the aisle to my right, one row ahead of me, sat a husky man, his balding head glistening with perspiration. A pretty, red-haired woman sat next to him, staring out the window and knitting. As a familiar-looking newsboy came by hawking papers, the man turned his profile towards me.

I knew that face!

I had seen his picture recently. I was sure of it!

Dumbfounded, I stood up and angled out into the aisle. The lady folded the inside section of the newspaper and fanned herself with it while the man intently studied its front page. "Excuse me, Sir," I said haltingly, "but aren't you Charles Darrow, the man who invented...."

... I saw the headline across the top of the page...

It read: Franklin Roosevelt Nominated on Fourth Ballot. Roosevelt's youthful picture appeared below the headline of the Philadephia Inquirer. My eyes focused on its date: July 2, 1932!

"Yes?" the man responded. "I am Charles Darrow. Have we met?"

I took a long look at him, then at the passengers on the train headed for The World's Playground. Darrow, too, was headed there — as were many, many more of us, more than he'd ever dream.

"I beg your pardon, sir — have we met?" he repeated.

"Oh, yes," I said smiling.

Good Luck!

Rich Uncle Pennybags

MONOPOLY®

© 1935 Parker Brothers

Official Tournament Score Sheet for *Long* Game

Player's Name _____

Address _____

Table Number _____

Round Number _____

Phone Number _____ Date _____

Tournament Title _____

Use Rules for LONG Game. 4 houses
required before purchasing a hotel.
A hotel is valued as 5 houses.

| Property | With No Buildings | | | With Buildings | | | | | | Money | | |
	Fully Owned	Mort-gaged	Property Asset W-out Buildings	With 1 House	With 2 Houses	With 3 Houses	With 4 Houses	With a Hotel	Property Asset With Buildings	Denomi-nation	Number Held	Cash Value
Atlantic Avenue	$260	$130		$410	$560	$710	$860	$1010		$1 Bills	$	$
B & O Railroad	200	100										
Baltic Avenue	60	30		110	160	210	260	310				
Boardwalk	400	200		600	800	1000	1200	1400				
Connecticut Avenue	120	60		170	220	270	320	370				
Electric Company	150	75								$5 Bills	$	$
Illinois Avenue	240	120		390	540	690	840	990				
Indiana Avenue	220	110		370	520	670	820	970				
Kentucky Avenue	220	110		370	520	670	820	970				
Marvin Gardens	280	140		430	580	730	880	1030		$10 Bills	$	$
Mediterranean Avenue	60	30		110	160	210	260	310				
New York Avenue	200	100		300	400	500	600	700				

Property							
North Carolina Avenue	300	150	500	700	900	1100	1300
Oriental Avenue	100	50	150	200	250	300	350
Pacific Avenue	300	150	500	700	900	1100	1300
Park Place	350	175	550	750	950	1150	1350
Pennsylvania Railroad	200	100					
Pennsylvania Avenue	320	160	520	720	920	1120	1320
Reading Railroad	200	100					
Short Line	200	100					
States Avenue	140	70	240	340	440	540	640
St. Charles Place	140	70	240	340	440	540	640
St. James Place	180	90	280	380	480	580	680
Tennessee Avenue	180	90	280	380	480	580	680
Ventnor Avenue	260	130	410	560	710	860	1010
Vermont Avenue	100	50	150	200	250	300	350
Virginia Avenue	160	80	260	360	460	560	660
Water Works	150	75					
Total $							Total $

$20 Bills	$	$
$50 Bills	$	$
$100 Bills	$	$
$500 Bills	$	$
		Total $

Property Assets Without Buildings	$
Property Assets With Buildings	$
Money	$
Grand Total	$

_____
Signature of Player

_____
Signature of Banker/Referee

_____
Signature of Notary Public

® PARKER BROTHERS

MONOPOLY®

© 1935 Parker Brothers

Official Tournament Score Sheet for *Long* Game

Player's Name _____

Address _____

Table Number _____

Round Number _____

Phone Number _____ Date _____

Tournament Title _____

Use Rules for LONG Game. 4 houses required before purchasing a hotel. A hotel is valued as 5 houses.

Property	With No Buildings			With Buildings						Money		
	Fully Owned	Mort-gaged	Property Asset W-out Buildings	With 1 House	With 2 Houses	With 3 Houses	With 4 Houses	With a Hotel	Property Asset With Buildings	Denom-ination	Number Held	Cash Value
Atlantic Avenue	$260	$130		$410	$560	$710	$860	$1010				
B & O Railroad	200	100								$1	$	$
Baltic Avenue	60	30		110	160	210	260	310		Bills		
Boardwalk	400	200		600	800	1000	1200	1400				
Connecticut Avenue	120	60		170	220	270	320	370				
Electric Company	150	75								$5	$	$
Illinois Avenue	240	120		390	540	690	840	990		Bills		
Indiana Avenue	220	110		370	520	670	820	970				
Kentucky Avenue	220	110		370	520	670	820	970				
Marvin Gardens	280	140		430	580	730	880	1030		$10	$	$
Mediterranean Avenue	60	30		110	160	210	260	310		Bills		
New York Avenue	200	100		300	400	500	600	700				

Property				500	700	900	1100	1300			
North Carolina Avenue	300	150		500	700	900	1100	1300	$20 Bills	$	$
Oriental Avenue	100	50		150	200	250	300	350			
Pacific Avenue	300	150		500	700	900	1100	1300			
Park Place	350	175		550	750	950	1150	1350			
Pennsylvania Railroad	200	100							$50 Bills	$	$
Pennsylvania Avenue	320	160		520	720	920	1120	1320			
Reading Railroad	200	100									
Short Line	200	100									
States Avenue	140	70		240	340	440	540	640	$100 Bills	$	$
St. Charles Place	140	70		240	340	440	540	640			
St. James Place	180	90		280	380	480	580	680			
Tennessee Avenue	180	90		280	380	480	580	680			
Ventnor Avenue	260	130		410	560	710	860	1010			
Vermont Avenue	100	50		150	200	250	300	350	$500 Bills	$	$
Virginia Avenue	160	80		260	360	460	560	660			
Water Works	150	75									
Total	$						Total	$		Total	$

Property Assets Without Buildings	$
Property Assets With Buildings	$
Money	$
Grand Total	$

Signature of Player

Signature of Banker/Referee

Signature of Notary Public

PARKER BROTHERS

MONOPOLY is Parker Brothers' registered trademark for its real estate trading game equipment.

PARKER BROTHERS

PRESENTS
CLASSIC
GAMES OF
STRATEGY
AND SKILL

The Family of MONOPOLY® Games...

In addition to our classic version, look for these keepsake editions for the avid MONOPOLY player:

• **1935 Commemorative Edition** is a replica of the original game, with re-issued tokens and game board, wooden houses, "grand" hotels, ivory-hued dice and a specially-written history of the game.

• **Deluxe Anniversary Edition** includes golden-tone tokens — plus a special anniversary MONOPOLY train, wooden houses and hotels, a specially-designed Banker's tray and Title Deed Card holder, and the special history.

ADVANCE TO BOARDWALK® hotel-building board game of high finance abounds with high rises and fast falls along the most famous — and expensive — piece of MONOPOLY real estate.

FREE PARKING® feed-the-meter game has Rich Uncle running errands, collecting points, and taking plenty of Second Chances.

The Family of CLUE® Games...

For 40 years, sleuths have endeavored to discover , where, and with what weapon? Look for these four versions:

CLUE® classic detective game asks, Was it Colonel Mustard in the Conservatory with the Revolver?

CLUE® MASTER DETECTIVE™ game for super sleuths is even more challenging, with more suspects, more rooms, more weapons.

CLUE® VCR and **CLUE II**™VCR games have more than one murder in every case as the famous — and infamous — suspects come to life on your TV.

The Family of BOGGLE® Games...

BOGGLE® and **BIG BOGGLE®** let everyone play at once, racing the timer to find the longest, highest-scoring words in the shake-up grid.

BOGGLE BOWL™ is head-to-head combat as players vie to make the longest words, two words, cross-words, even the most words, then issue a 10-second challenge.

Plus these challenging games...

RISK® world conquest game is the military strategy classic.

PENTE® game of skill proves the more you play, the better it gets!

Ask for these Parker Brothers games of strategy at your favorite game department.